SALES PEOPLE THINK THEY KNOW EVERYTHING

(Proven Strategies to Put More Money
in Your Pocket Tomorrow!)

Chris Lovett

First Edition

Fulton Books
Meadville, PA

Published by Fulton Books 2022

ISBN 979-8-88505-161-3 (paperback)
ISBN 979-8-88505-162-0 (digital)

Printed in the United States of America

For
Stephanie,
Evan,
Bryce,
Jacob,
Avery,
Aiden,
Baylee,
May each of you find your dreams.

Contents

Acknowledgments

This book would have never happened without the thousands of participants I have had the privilege of working with over the last thirty years. You have all taught me something in your own unique ways.

I must acknowledge the best sales person, trainer, mentor, and speaker I have ever seen: John J. Gehegan. Many of the concepts in this book are derived directly from him. I have learned and put into practice what was taught to me by him. I have become very successful in what I do because I put these lessons into practice. I now have the privilege of passing many of mine and these on to you, the reader. He practices what he preaches, and although he would downplay it humbly, he is extremely successful. Thank you, John, for your example, your belief in me, and everything you've taught and continued to teach me.

I also must recognize my wife, Stephanie. She has also had a long successful career in sales. She has been my sounding board, my editor, and my supporter. She has stayed on me persistently to get this done, and not because she is my wife. She believes in it as a sales person. Thank you, Stephanie, for your loyal and unbiased help. You are the best sale I ever made.

Preface

Over the course of thirty years and thousands of sales representatives trained from all over the world, I have been asked many times, "When are you going to write a book?" Flattered, I would answer humbly, "Oh, I don't know if what I have to say would make that big of difference." Or if I was in a little more assertive mode, I would say, "I'm going to start one soon!" It sure was nice of those people to ask and, in many instances, encourage me to do so. I thought about it off and on for a few years but never put a serious mind to it.

During this time of "thinking about it," I read a few new sales books during my travels. I read some really good ones. I revisited one I had read many years prior. I also read a few that I thought were pretty, well, bad. Let me be clear, after the process I have gone through to write this book, I will now never ever call someone's book "bad." This took countless thoughts and work and time away from family and other things to get this done.

In reflection, the other sales books I read were not "bad," but they were, for me, heavy. Not that I was lacking the cognitive ability to comprehend the material; they just seemed to have lots of charts and graphs and statistics and theories. The research that was done in them was tremendous, and I actually learned a ton of things I didn't know before the consumption of the information. But the question that kept recurring in my mind was "Is there any value in a sales book that was simple?" What if I wrote a book that salespeople could read, and their first thoughts were, "I've been there," "I used to do it that way," "I've never tried saying it that way," and "I'm going to ask that question at my three-o'clock meeting this afternoon!"

So the premise was born. You won't be getting tons of graphs and charts and theoretical learning from this book. I have not researched the perfect six key words to say in a sales presentation. I have found for me that experiential learning is way more effective than theoretical learning. For example, you can role-play with colleagues all you want, but they know what you know and they know what you're supposed to and going to say back. The outcome is somewhat known. When you walk into a sales presentation and go live, it is a totally different learning experience. There is nothing wrong with roleplay by the way. It does teach you, in theory, what to do. Nothing beats the real thing.

So I wanted to give you the real thing. This book is both journal and guide. These chapters explore a life in sales. It is full of real-life experiences I have had as a sales representative, a sales and district manager, a corporate trainer, and an executive with a thirty-seven-year firm in the financial sector. I wanted to take each chapter as a walk down the road of the sales process. You will find, hopefully, some interesting experiences that apply directly to components of the sales method and the application to each piece. These are just my opinions and advice. Optimistically, I wanted this to be simple in format, to give you real-life examples and ideas that you could immediately put into play in the field or your other arenas of sales. Will everything I share with you be perfect and work every time? Does anyone know anything that does? My goal is to share with you what I have learned that has made me quite successful and that, in some small way, will help you easier achieve the goals and dreams you have set before you.

Chapter 1

The Fuel to Start

The summers in Kansas City, Missouri, are beautiful. There is double the number of sunny days than cloudy, and the average temperature is only 76 degrees. Between flowering dogwood trees and striking Azalea bushes, Kansas City has more miles of boulevards than Paris and more fountains than any city except Rome. With a thriving metro population of nearly 2.1 million people, Kansas City is a city of diverse economic opportunities, great professional sports, and world-famous barbeque.

It was here that I met Lance Mitchell. As the corporate sales trainer, I had flown into Kansas City to work with their sales team for the week. My typical schedule would be to spend Monday in the office, conducting a day-long sales meeting with all the sales representatives. For the rest of the week, I would work each day out in the field with a sales rep that the district manager felt needed some guidance, assistance, or, in some cases, just plain encouragement. After I finished the Monday meeting, the DM and I met to go over the reps I would be working with and a little background on their performance and possible areas of direction. Tuesday was Sally "needs help cold-calling" Kennedy. Wednesday was Ronaldo "talks too much" Diaz. Thursday was Jackie "discounter" Lang. He then paused and said, "Now, on Friday. You'll be working with Lance." He then got up, came around his desk, put his hand on my shoulder, looked me in the eye, and said, "Make sure you get a lot of rest Thursday evening. You'll need it."

Lance and I decided to meet at 7:30 a.m., Friday morning, at Scooter's Coffee House on Walnut Street. We didn't meet there for the coffee, but since it was in the Town Pavilion, it gave us lots of options of where to leave my car so I could ride with Lance for our day in the field. When I pulled up, Lance was standing in front of his car. He was wearing a crisp blue suit and sipping on some sort of homemade fruit smoothie. During our Monday sales meeting, he sat near the back and didn't talk much, so I didn't know really what to expect, and here I was, about to find out.

We greeted each other, and he made a quick apology for the condition of the inside of his car. As I finished fastening the seatbelt, I began to ask Lance what the plan of our day was to be. He raised his hand up as if to silence me, and said, "Hold on a second, I have to do something first." He then reached to the side panel of his door and pulled out two CDs. (For my younger audience, CDs were how we listened to music in the car before Apple and Samsung and others made it digital!)

Without saying another word, he loaded the first CD into the slot. Within seconds, the song "Fuel" by Metallica, off their *Reload* album, was blaring through the speakers. Lance was channeling every member of the band. One minute, he's singing along with James Hetfield at the top of his lungs, the next minute he's banging the steering wheel as if Lars Ulrich's drum set had been teleported to his vehicle. I ventured once, right after the first verse, to cut in and ask Lance again about our day. But with eyes closed and his head bobbing left and right, he raised his hand with the "wait" signal. He was clearly in the middle of the moment, and I began to remember what the district manager had said to me.

When the decibels finally subsided, I returned to the question of what our day was to be, and again, his hand went up one more time to the "hold-on-please" signal. He retrieved a second CD and jammed it into the slot. In moments, the theme of the movie *Rocky* ("Gonna Fly Now") began filling the car. You know what happened next? I sat there and was witness to some of the best air boxing I have ever seen before or since. When "Gonna Fly Now" was fading away,

Lance snapped back to reality, ejected Rocky from the player, turned his head my direction, and said, "Now I'm ready!"

My initial reaction to this kid was to take him to the nearest psyche ward to see if he was mentally stable. I mean what I just experienced was crazy! However, the moment the music was over, Lance rattled off his schedule for the day. Guess what? He was booked solid with *appointments* for most of the day. He had two *appointments* scheduled before noon and two after noon. He also had a *specific* place between the two sets of *appointments* that he wanted to spend some time prospecting in person. As the day wore on and our conversation grew, I brought it back to that "ritual" I had observed just outside of Scooter's. And he said, "Those two songs fire me up. It's as simple as that. It's hard out here in the weeds. Between the prospects and my competitors, I'm constantly getting pushed and challenged every day. Those two songs give me the *fuel* to get my attitude off to a positive, motivating start."

On the plane ride back to corporate, I thought about the hundreds of sales representatives I had worked with over the years. I learned that I could count on one hand the number who seemed to have some sort of *fuel* that started their day. Not coffee, not some energy drink, but that quenching of the "attitude thirst"—that "fill up" of the positive spirit.

As a corporate trainer, most of my time spent with sales representatives in the field was on the fun part of the sales process: the appointment! It's not too hard to get geared up for a day full of people willing to meet with you! Not many reps, at least the smarter ones, were going to drag the "corporate guy" all over the city with nothing but cold calling on the day's agenda. The smart ones, the successful ones, had a good mixture of both the prospecting and the fruit of that labor, the appointment. I was reminded of that daily grind, that incessant search for that next lead, that next referral, that next meeting, and that next sale. The grind is definitely challenging and daunting. It's harder than most people think. Lance's moment of fueling himself in his own unique way was so innocent in its form, and yet, so poignant. Ironically, it refueled me! Sure, the job is tough—most rewarding ones are! So gas up. Let's go sell something!

Where Do You Need Fuel?

It's hard to be successful in any one area of life if all, or some of the other areas, are out of sync or out of rhythm. When you are on the job, do issues at home distract you? While trying to enjoy quality and much-needed family time, do you worry about issues on the job? Do you worry about your finances while at the gym, working on your health? If the answer is yes to some of these scenarios, then you are probably in good company. Life now is more complex, faster, harder, and growing in complication and technological advances to keep up with it all! So where do I fuel, you ask? For the sake of over simplification—fuel everywhere! In fact, try to *F*ind *U*topia in your *E*ntire *L*ife.

The definition of utopia is an ideal and perfect place or state where everyone lives in harmony, and *everything* is for the *best.* While the state of utopia is perfection and a never-ending quest, the ideal of utopia can be a daily exercise! In no way do I possess the education necessary to offer scientific method on how to exercise the emotional, spiritual, intellectual, and physical wellness areas of your life. I do, however, have about thirty years of experience being around and working with thousands of sales representatives and sales managers all over North America. My observations are, of course, in no way absolutes, but the vast majority of the most successful sales reps I've ever been around seem to be diligently working on FUEL.

I would bet that in my tenure managing sales and service personnel over these several years, I have spent as much time counseling them on personal issues as I have in helping them increase their sales production. I have heard more stories of boyfriends and girlfriends, husbands and wives, problems with kids, and worked with them through health issues and unfortunate family tragedies. I've counseled on furthering education, getting finances in order, which house to buy, and whether they should have a dog or a cat! Of course, I'm happy to offer my help and way under qualified opinions on much of these subjects because I cared about my team members. But for some, and more than you might think, their problems distracted them too much for them to overcome it and succeed in their profession and, worse, their family life. A smaller group of them tended to be the type that just seemed resigned to live a life of constant drama and turmoil. I only added to the turmoil when I had to excuse them from their duties. The less drama and turmoil within a sales organization, the more successful the sales organization.

We live in a society where instant gratification is the norm. When I first started in sales, I listened to my Brian Tracy cassette tapes in my car! I had to occasionally find a pay phone and call into the office to get messages. I had to get directions from my prospects on how to get to their offices! Now the phone that I wear as a watch does all of that and orders dinner for me to be there when I get home! We are more conditioned to have it now. I think that somehow correlates to job searching and the decision-making process of choosing a profession in the first place. It's so easy to go on a host of job search engines and see what's out there.

Who is hiring now? What can I get fast? Well, what happened to "What do I *want* to do? What *skills* do I have? What skills can I *learn?* What makes me *happy*, and can I do it and get paid for it? What am I *good* at, and who needs *someone like me*?"

We, unfortunately, live in a kind of "try-it-out" state of mind, and I certainly feel that sometimes you do have to try something to see if it fits you. But it becoming the rule, instead of the exception to the rule, is watering down the people staying and performing at a high level in a profession with any longevity.

So what happens? Companies have a higher turnover rate and hiring from a pool of candidates contributing to the chances of higher turnover rate. Seems like a recipe for disaster and a waste of a lot of money. I think if more people spent more time critically thinking about the profession they really want to be in and how they can be successful in that field, might be the foundation to a successful career. Utopia has to have a cornerstone.

So the search for fuel can continue. I was conducting a seminar in Manhattan recently, and one of the first attendees arrived immediately put his stuff on the table, opened his laptop, and started to login. It was 7:15 a.m. In moments, he was frantically searching through papers, looking though his phone, and growing a bit frustrated. I asked if everything was okay. He said, "Oh yes, everything's all right." But then told me that his boss had sent him an email at 3:15 a.m. this morning and needed an answer by 8:00 a.m. I finished setting up my materials and equipment for the session and thought to myself, *Wow. Why is someone sending an email at 3:15 a.m.?* That is not anywhere near utopia. Then expecting an employee to have an answer in less than five hours. That's not the employee's utopia.

Here is a crazy thought. What if we worked harder with our families at home and harder with our associates at work? What if the balance was there? With everyone. What would that do for production? What would that do for us at home? Are there exceptions that come up? Well, sure. Are there "work emergencies?" Of course. But all the time? Someone once said, "Work hard and play hard." I kind of agree. Work hard at work. Play hard away from work. When there is balance between the two, the two are more likely to get the attention they deserve.

Not long after the attendee struggling with his boss' email had arrived, another attendee came into the room. I said to him, "Good morning!" Without batting an eye, he responded, "Every morning is a good morning!" I asked him why? He said, "I have a beautiful wife, two great kids, a job that's happy to have me, and I just left my 5:30 a.m. kickboxing class!" Now this is the exaggeration of the point with a capital E, but that young man was one of the most engaging and interesting attendees of the tens of thousands I have trained!

I've learned some powerful words in the sales process. One of my favorites is the word "make." It is extremely different than the word "find." I've observed that most of the successful people I've met live in the world of make. (And not make-believe, ha!) For example, they make time instead of find time. They make time to do the things that can help them be more productive and successful. They also make plans. They make changes. I've heard salespeople say around the office that "I just couldn't find time today to make prospecting calls." Really? Of course, you *couldn't*, or should I say *wouldn't*? See, the successful ones made the time.

How does this relate to our FUEL? My thought is you have to make the time to do the things both in your career and home. Make yourself put the phone down and play with the kids at home! Make yourself pick-up the phone and call prospects at work and check the emails later! Make the time to uncover what can start you off and keep you in "fuel" throttle for each day!

What is it that motivates you the best to start your day? Is it of the cerebral, or is it of the physical? Is it something else? Is it your favorite breakfast? A morning workout at the gym? Could it be a playlist of songs that just simply fire you up and put a smile on your face? Start there. Make the time for something that fuels the start of your day in the field because you're going to need it! Then put some fuel in *all* the areas of your life where you can! Baby steps. Proactively, start to look for ways to change it up! As best you can, look for balance. Keep your attention on them all. And when it comes to the work, when you start as many days as you can with fuel for thought and a balance in the core aspects of your life, you've given yourself a head start to being the successful sales person you know you are!

Chapter 2

Your Universe of Opportunities

After three decades of working closely with sales professionals, both in the field and in classroom settings, a consistent theme appeared with the majority of them. They seemed to be more reactive when it came to hunting that next sale versus being *proactive* in hunting it.

If the organization provided leads to them, they were quite good at going out and securing that business. If the referral managed to *make its way to them*, they were quite happy to hop in their car and go try to close the deal. The warmer the lead or introduction, the easier they went about trying to make it happen.

But when the referrals ran dry, or the leads were slow that week or that month, their success began to falter. The panic began to set in! Instead of owning it, they would be at their sales manager's door asking where the leads were and why weren't they coming in?

It reminds me of the classic sales movie *Glen Gary Glen Ross.* This 1993 film is focused on a group of real-estate salespeople. The team isn't doing too well, and a representative from headquarters is sent to figure out what's going on. In fact, it turns out to be more of a threat to keep their jobs than a motivational, encouraging visit.

One of the main characters, played by the late Jack Lemon, is frustrated that he isn't getting the "good leads," the "Glen Gary leads." His point to his sales manager is that if he had the better leads, he could close more business because the leads he was currently working were not any good. The dilemma for him in the movie is that the "good" leads are only going to go to the people that close the "other" leads.

He then exacerbates the problem by trying to pressure the people that he is currently working and falls deeper into a dark and tragic place. If Jack had reached out into the entire universe of opportunities instead of relying on only one part of it, he may have turned his fortune around in time to steal the grand-prize Cadillac away from Al Pacino.

Are You Taking Advantage of Your Universe of Opportunity?

This universe consists of the five main opportunities to attract and secure your next sale: referrals, mailings, cold calling, networking, and outbound calling. Some sales professionals excel in one part of the universe while others succeed elsewhere in the universe.

Some feel they are better "face-to-face." Some feel the referral route is the best route. Some people hate making a cold phone call. A problem arises if their "area" of the universe dries up or becomes stale. This is often experienced after a particularly successful month.

If the sales representative can't thrive in or doesn't even utilize the other areas of the universe, it creates a problem that many representatives find themselves in constantly. In my experiences, I have met several very successful sales professionals who do an outstanding job using the entire universe.

They end up working harder and smarter than the rest, and they are usually the ones walking up on the stage to receive their award, their big bonus, and learn the location of the exotic resort that the President's Gold Circle Club will be held that year! Of course, they'll be going! Why aren't you?

Universe Area No. 1—Referrals

There is no argument that the best way to your next new customer is through the referral of one of your happy existing customers. It is the warmest of introductions. Since a peer has recommended you or introduced you, there is already some degree of underlying trust already established. The defenses are lowered, and all you have to do is go in there and not foul it up! Great, right? No wonder this is the most preferred and happiest part of the universe. Cue the unicorns and the rainbows.

Reality check, please! I want you to think of your sales day yesterday. Tell you what, think of your entire last *week*. How many of your customers called you up with hot new leads for you? How many prospects showed up at your office, telling you that they were sent there by one of your clients? Ten? Twenty? Two? How about zero. Would it shock you that almost 75 percent of the sales representatives I have sat in appointments with *failed* to ask for a referral? And this part of the universe is the one I hear most salespeople say they rely on to get their deals, and *also*, as an excuse not to cold call or pick up a phone!

Well, there are two ways to improve your success in this part of the universe. First, *start asking for them*. As I mentioned before, I have sat with hundreds of salespeople during hundreds of appointments with existing clients and potential prospects. The sizeable majority failed to ask the person sitting across from them to help them find their next appointment. Many of them were solely focused on the task at hand, which was making sure they executed the appointment in the best possible way to get the next step moving forward or even getting the deal. And, let's be honest, that is what they should be doing!

I have watched some very talented salespeople do amazing presentations and flawless navigation of the appointment. I've walked into places with sales reps where we were almost thrown out at first, only for the owner to be signing the agreement forty-five minutes later. In almost every instance, once the owner said yes and the deal was done, we were gone! We would often walk back to the car, excited about what had just occurred, and then drove over to the next building and walk in there *cold*. What a mistake. We were making the job harder, even after a victory.

I've often wondered why the request for a referral never happened. One theory is that the focus of the "in-the-moment" appointment would take precedent in the sales person's mind and cause him to actually forget about asking for a referral. Another theory, which is one that I swear I felt I could literally sense, was that the sales person, regardless if the appointment was a success or failure, felt internally that she had kept the decision maker too long in the meeting: *especially* after a successful one, where the decision maker would be involved signing agreements, retrieving financials, etc. The thought of asking for more, in this case a referral, was too much.

When I would ask them later why they didn't, they would say that "they didn't want to push their luck." This wasn't limited to unknown prospects; the same reaction would come sitting across from someone who was *already their client*! The very person who already believed in them and their product or service, they were afraid they were bothering them for something more. So guess what? At the end of your meeting with any client or potential, ask for a referral. Period.

Second, when you start asking for referrals, *ask for them accurately*. The problem most salespeople unknowingly encounter when they actually ask for them is, they do it wrong. Think about how you ask for referrals. What is it you normally say? Is it this: "Do you know anyone else who could use our services?" Not bad, right? At least you're trying! The problem is the question is too big for the person receiving it. The question is too ambiguous.

When the person hears this question, their mental rolodex scrolls back all the way to third grade, and the names start spinning forward. In all the clutter of names, the person probably answers you with this standard response, "I can't think of anyone right now, but give me some time and leave me a few of your business cards, and if I come up with any, I'll let you know." *And how long have you been waiting?*

The question is too generic. So let's get it more specific. Let's say you are a rep in mid-town Manhattan. You need questions that get your client out of space, onto planet Earth, in North America, in the United States, in New York, in Manhattan, and onto Fifty-Seventh Street and Fifth Avenue. "Ms. Client, do you happen to know the owner of Books and Coffee across the street? Would you be able to introduce me?" "Mr. Prospect, I have not had the pleasure of meeting your accountant. May I meet her?" "Ms. Customer of Mine, who are your three best vendors? May I get their information from you? I would love to talk to them about what we do." The more specific the request is, the more likely you get a name.

Do they know anyone else? They know lots and lots of people; it's too generic! Do they know the owners of businesses *around them*? Those, they can quickly name.

Lastly, when it comes to asking for referrals, one small part of the sales process that is powerful throughout is asking questions. We will delve more into the immense value it brings to your results a little later, but as it relates to referrals, try something new. In your next appointment and the ones that follow, don't end it until you ask for a referral. Make sure you do it. Make it specific. Make it help you be more successful.

Universe Area No. 2—Mailings: Email and Beyond

"Neither snow nor rain nor heat nor gloom of night stays these couriers from the swift completion of their appointed rounds." Although not the official creed of the post office, it is most associated with the American postmen and women. The good people at the post office do a great job *delivering the mail*; the problem is with the ones *reading* and *responding* to the mail. The general consensus of the response rate pertaining to mail outs is 1 percent. So math majors, you send one hundred letters or flyers out, how many responded? That's right, one. She isn't even the one that will buy it; she just responded to take a look.

While mass mailings are going to be part of any company's advertising strategy, depending on it to be a major part of your sales success is a mistake. Blanket-type mailings are generic and impersonal. We, the people, instantly pick up on that. Why is it that almost everyone knows what a "form letter" is?

Knowing there are some individuals who will always respond to anything, a better practice is to send a smaller number of letters to a more targeted group. Pick three or four companies you are really wanting to partner with, or three to five companies that maybe you've struggled getting in front of using other areas of the universe and send them the correspondence. Keep it simple. Your initial goal is to schedule the appointment anyway.

The outline of your letter should be a quick introduction, a brief benefit statement for setting up the appointment, and at the conclusion, add a specific day and time on which you will follow back to start a dialogue. When you are sending a smaller sample out, the easier it is to track and keep up with the follow-up.

The follow-up is what's critical. It is imperative that when you write that you will call her Friday at 9:15 a.m. to get her opinion on exploring a business relationship, then Friday at 9:15 a.m., her phone should be ringing. (By the way, an advantage of saying you will call her at 9:15 a.m. in your email is it can help you with the gatekeeper! "Is she expecting your call?" Then you get to say, "Yes. I told her I would be contacting her today at this time.")

One of the first building blocks in business is trust. And this is a small first example that they even may not pick up consciously, that you do what you say you're going to do. Keeping a smaller targeted few aids you in being successful at following up. I've met and worked with salespeople who have sent letters certified. They paid a small fee to guarantee that their intended recipient *signed* for it. I've done that a few times myself, and it worked.

If the reward of the intended prospect's business is worth the risk, get creative. Overnight a package with some advertisement and include a handwritten note. Do something that stands out among the others vying for his business. You don't have to break the bank to get creative.

The tips here ring true for email and the various channels of communication that pop up every day. In your emails, follow the same outline. Add a link to your company's website where all they have to do is click and surf. If you're using sites like LinkedIn or other business contact sites, consider upgrading the best level to get you access to your prospects. The adage is so true, especially in advertising yourself and your company: you have to spend a little money to make a little money. Whatever channel you use in this part of the universe, keep it targeted, keep it brief, be creative, and follow up!

Universe Area No. 3—Cold Calling

How many people wake up in the morning and say to themselves, "Hey, I want to walk in on complete strangers in the middle of their workday and try to sell them stuff?" Other than a very few super type A individuals, most of the rest of us don't particularly care for it. I wonder why? Cold calling in Manhattan on January 7 is *literally* cold calling. Cold calling in Orlando on July 27 is *literally* the opposite of cold calling. I think the best place to cold-call would be Maui. But I'll bet even the sales reps that work the beautiful Hawaiian Isles hate it as much as those of us on the mainland do.

I've even read sales books, some by pretty famous sales gurus, calling for the end of cold calling! Cold calling, in and of itself, is not to be hated. The problem lies with the fact that most salespeople do two things wrong. One, they are cold calling to <u>get</u> appointments instead of <u>around</u> their appointments. Two, they are quite simply doing it wrong.

When starting your job with any outside sales organization, there is no doubt that initially you may have to get out there and beat the streets to find possible prospects with whom to start trying to work. To stay in this area of the universe as your main source of lead generation will cause you to burn out quick. I can't think of a single one, of all the most successful salespeople I've had the privilege to work with or manage, that constantly beat the streets in person all day.

Other than tiresome, they knew there's only so many people you can reach out to in one day—in person. As you begin to master all the areas of the universe, you will find that cold calling before or after already scheduled appointments is the most effective use of your time.

Right now, recall the last appointment that you had. You arrived at the decision maker's business. What did you do? Were you early? If so, what did you do? You probably looked over your notes and your prepared material and got your head straight before going in. Okay. Not bad. You go in. Guess what? Great meeting! She wants to work with you.

You're leaving the business now. What did you do? Many salespeople make a critical activity error at this very moment. They rush back to the office to celebrate the new possible deal! So what's wrong with that, you might ask? I would submit to you that your confidence level is at a major high point after a great appointment and at its highest when you just closed a deal.

Don't immediately drive off into the sunset! Use that rush of adrenaline and confidence and walk into a minimum of three businesses right there around that prospect you just met with. With that swagger that comes in the midst of a great sales moment, go in and try to get to the owner. Worst case, you can gather the necessary information to prospect again later. I have seen countless examples of this bringing forth amazing results. If you are selling to a segment where the size of business you call on isn't realistic to be nearby, consider aiming that energy to your new prospect and ask for some specific referrals before you leave the meeting. Remember, most of your competitor salespeople don't do it.

Another valuable time to cold-call is when the appointment doesn't go your way, or worse, the decision makers pull no-shows. There are three scenarios that happen when you show up for your appointment. 1) They are there, and you have the meeting. 2) They pull a no-show. 3) They are there, and you have the appointment but quickly realize they are not a prospect. Let's assume your initial appointment with a potential prospect runs about forty-five minutes.

<u>In the first scenario</u>, you have the meeting; the outcome is good, and you set up next steps to move them forward in the process. After the meeting ends, you make it a point to visit a minimum of three businesses nearby. Bonus points to any of you who ask the person you were just meeting with if he or she knows the decision makers near his or her location. That way, you already have the name of who you are looking for when you cold-call.

<u>In the second scenario</u>, your appointment pulls the dreaded no-show. Let's acknowledge that there are three types of no-shows. Type 1 is the legit no-show. Your appointment isn't there because he has a real dilemma. His child is sick and needs to be picked up from school. She has a client crisis and has been called off to assist in its resolution. Some unintended circumstance has caused the mix up. So what now?

Well first, he owes you. You were there; he wasn't. People with any sliver of moral compass will know that and reschedule. And because of their legitimate reason, I would have no problem working something out for a reschedule. But at the moment, there is not going to be an appointment. Guess what you do for the next forty-five minutes? You spend it cold calling right there in that part of the field. You scheduled your time to be at that appointment for at least forty-five minutes, so don't drive back to your office dejected; get out there and meet new potential customers. They're waiting for you. By the way, if you don't, who else might?

Type 2 is the chaotic no-show. Your appointment isn't there because she just plainly forgot about it. She didn't write it down. He thought it was tomorrow. He meant to call you to reschedule, but it slipped his mind. It wasn't intentional, but some decision makers aren't the most organized. This should be one that is easily rescheduled too, but you might want to send an invite, call to confirm, or show up an hour early for the next one. So what now? I think you know the answer. You now have a fresh forty-five minutes to find someone to work. Type 3 is the shun no-show. This is the person who purposely blows you off. This is the one who tells you he'll meet with you on Friday at 2:00 p.m., and when you show up, the receptionist tells you he left for vacation on Wednesday. We have all had this happen to us.

The question I would ask myself is, Would I want this person as a client? I have a lot of examples of people who treat you bad when they don't know you and treat you worse when they do. My advice would be to find someone else to work with. You have a spare forty-five minutes; get to it!

<u>The last scenario</u> is the appointment that is over quick. You arrive excited for the meeting, but after a few minutes into the conversation, it becomes apparent that this person is not a prospect, and your meeting ends early. Your forty-five-minute meeting turned into a fifteen-minute meeting. Well, what should we do with that extra thirty minutes? I think you know what to do.

Secondly, whenever the brave tries to cold-call, they might not be as effective as they could be. Here is what I've heard a lot of people say. They walk in the business and find the first person they see and say, "Hi, I'm Joe Salesguy, and I was wondering if the owner was around? I work for ABC company and want to share a little about what we do. Um, are you the owner? Is there an owner or manager I could talk to?" Yikes! Painful. Can you be any more awkward? The problem here is you are sending so many signals that you're not expected, calling on him out of the blue, and you are begging to be screened out.

Think for a moment what you say when you actually have *an already scheduled appointment.* You probably walk in, find the greeting employee, and say, "Hi. I'm Joe, I'm here to see Kristen. I have an 11:00 with her." The person then goes and notifies Kristen that her appointment is here. Use the same psychology to your advantage on a cold call. Walk in, find the greeting employee and say, "Hi. I'm Joe. I'm *here to see* the owner." Use the same tone you would if the appointment already existed. Bonus points for those who actually Google a name before they walk in. "Hi. I'm Joe Johnson. I'm here to see Kristen Jacobson." Confident, not arrogant. Assertive, not aggressive. This simple tweak works.

Cold calling is always considered one of the most daunting parts of the universe. Used effectively, it can be one of the most rewarding. I'm going to prove that to you in an upcoming chapter! It is one part of the universe where your sales skills get sharpened the fastest. When you get good at walking into a business cold, navigating the receptionist/gatekeeper screens, reaching the decision maker, getting a meeting, and closing the sale, you become a very well-rounded sales person.

Often in my career I have gotten this question: Would you rather have the world's greatest "closer" or the world's greatest "prospector" on your sales team? My answer is this: I would love to have both. But forced to choose, give me the one who prospects without abandon, for he or she will become the better salesperson. If you come to the end of your month and you need two more to hit your goal and you only have two prospects close, then you need to be the world's greatest closer. However, if you come to the end of the month and you need two more to hit your goal and you have twelve prospects close, you don't need to be the world's greatest closer. Start cold calling around all of your appointments. It is guaranteed that you will find more people to work.

Universe Area No. 4—Networking

One of the most misused parts of the universe is in the area of networking. People invest lots of money and time in trade shows, charity events, job fairs, networking groups, and mixers. After a hard day at work, they run to the rotary meeting to shake a few hands. While better than doing nothing, the effectiveness of your networking is your primary standard on how and when to do it. In Malcom Gladwell's book, *The Tipping Point*, he identifies three types of people that aid something moving from average through the tipping point to where it boons. The three types are mavens, salespeople, and the connectors. The connector is one who has a knack for meeting and getting to know people in all types of business circles. Gladwell defines a real connector as someone who has social networks of over one hundred people. A key to you achieving your goals exponentially beyond your wildest dreams is to become quite effective in the connector domain.

There are two main areas of the universe of networking: virtually and in person.

The first recognizable social media site, Six Degrees, was created in 1997. It enabled users to upload a profile and make friends with other users. In 1999, the first blogging sites became popular, creating the beginning of a social-media sensation. In August 2003, a group of employees working together on another platform came up with the idea of My Space.

On February 4, 2004, a Harvard student and his roommates launched something called Facebook. The business sector wasn't going to miss out. Considered the leader in business networking, LinkedIn was launched in 2002. Now there are dozens upon dozens of networking business sites like Salesforce, Zoominfo, Partner Up, and Ryze—just to name a few.

Your company and you are your brand. So get yourself out there! Reach out to all types of people because you never know what doors may open. Spending some quality time in this virtual part of the universe allows you to meet people you would never have the chance to meet beating the streets. Not only are there future prospects out there, but also connecting with fellow sales professionals, exchanging ideas and challenges, can do nothing but boost your sales skills and acumen. Don't be afraid and spend a little money to upgrade to some of the premium features these sites provide. Features like real phone numbers and specific email addresses get you in contact with the people you need to get as audience. The more billboards you can put up of yourself and your company, the better the attention you might receive.

Earlier, I outlined some strategies on cold calling, which, in a sense, is also networking. Strengthen your best quality of in-person, face-to-face communication by joining some local business sources like the Rotary, Chamber of Commerce, BNI groups, and even groups like the Toastmasters. Sharpen your presentation skills that help you when you have to deliver proposals to large groups of decision makers. The leadership growth you will achieve is invaluable.

Over the many years of working with salespeople, I have encouraged them to join associations. Almost every business type has one. There are car-dealer associations, doctor associations, manufacturer associations. Contact the president of these associations. Do you know what keeps the presidents of associations up at night? Finding a guest speaker to speak at their next meeting. Offer yourself up to speak at the next one. This isn't a commercial for your company, and let them know that. But you can give a fifteen-minute talk on what you do; it helps the members of that association.

If you are a banker, what about fifteen minutes on how banks approve business owners for equipment loans? What is the process? How long does it take? What do they need to know? What do they have to supply? If you sell data processing or storage, how does that work? What are the things most businesses need to store and how does it save them money to do so? If you sell in the merchant services industry, what are the new technologies being used? What is going on in the payments industry? How are merchants protecting themselves from fraud, write-offs, or collections? Remember, this is not a commercial. This is giving them something that might help them. The best part is you just happen to be the maven of the subject. On breaks and lunch, many of the attendees might have questions, and you have the answers. Now insert your commercial.

Finally, a number of your current customers are probably already members of their respective associations. Just a thought, ask to tag along at the next meeting. There is nothing better than a happy customer introducing you to all her peers. In an ever-changing world of social media and changes in the marketplace, stay relevant. Stay knowledgeable. Stay visible.

Universe Area No. 5—Outbound Calling

How many people wake up in the morning, their feet hit the floor, and they say, "Hey, let's pick up the phone and call complete strangers and try to sell them stuff?" I'm going to guess that number is infinitesimally small. Other than a very few crazy people, most dread cold calling over the phone. One's own experience with telemarketers and unsolicited phone calls brings a certain psychological barrier when the one has to do it.

There are many excuses why people don't like it: It's not personal. People are rude. I don't know what they're going to say. The results are not worth the time and effort. Still, today, using the phone as a prospecting tool is by far the most efficient and effective area of the universe of opportunities. Let's have a contest. I'm going to challenge you in a prospecting battle. I will choose the phone and you go out and cold-call. We're all better face-to-face, right?

Well, I've made ten dials before you get to your car. I've made fifteen more while you're driving to the area you want to cold-call. I've probably called five more before you shake the hand of the first gatekeeper. Get the picture? So how do we diffuse the nerves of using the phone? It's actually quite simple. Keep it simple!

My dear friend and mentor, John Gehegan, owner and founder of Gehegan & Associates in San Diego, California, instilled in me the principles to make this the most successful area of my prospecting universe. His firm has been working with salespeople in the financial world for over thirty-eight years. He has literally traveled the globe teaching people his proven method for being successful over the phone. He didn't reinvent the wheel. He made the wheel better!

Be prepared. Most people are underprepared before they call a business. Taking the time to find the name of the decision maker is the first critical step. That sounds pretty logical, right? I wish you could have listened to some of the calls I have listened to over the years. How's this for an opening line, and have you been guilty too? "Hi. My name is Chris, and I work for ABC company. I was just wondering who would be the person that makes the decisions around there? Is there an owner? Or president? Are you the owner, or president? Who do I talk to that might be interested in this new piece of technology that...blah...blah...blah?" And we wonder why we struggle with gatekeepers.

You have to know that Jason Wright is the one you want, and when the person answers the phone at the company you are prospecting, you are calling directly for him. You also need to know revenue size, length of time in business, number of employees, locations, headquarters. There are dozens of sites that help you acquire this information. Many are free! Find them and use them.

Most people don't understand a very simple statistic that is hurting them before they even dial the number. Sixty-six percent of people you try to reach off any given list at any given time are not available. Two-thirds. So if you don't make enough phone calls, it doesn't matter how good you are because you won't reach as many people with whom to talk.

I've heard reps say that they have four or five really good prospects they're going to call today. Guess what? Even if they are horrible prospects, almost four of the five won't be on the other end of the call. Unfortunately, the one you do reach is quite happy with her current provider. So what do you have now, Bob? Nothing! In a thirty-minute calling block, a good rule of thumb is to have about twenty names on the list. Statistically, that should leave you between six and eight people to have a conversation. An excellent goal would be to close an average of <u>*two*</u> of them for a meeting.

When calling the prospect, oftentimes, a classic mistake most salespeople make is, they lose focus on the purpose of the call. The goal on the initial call is singular: set the appointment. There are no exceptions to this goal. The person is not even a prospect yet. The person right now is only a suspect. Suspects get scheduled. Only after you and he determine you might work together *at* the appointment does he get product, service, and pricing information. Not before. Prospects get pricing.

So after you introduce yourself, make sure it's a good time to proceed; give them a good opening benefit statement about what your company excels at doing and ask for the meeting. Keep it short and clear on purpose. Three scenarios exist after that. 1) He agrees to the appointment. 2) He objects to the appointment. 3) He wants you to tell him more right now. The last one is the dangerous one. You don't even know for sure if he would be a viable prospect yet. So easily explain that many of your clients have found that a face-to-face meeting gives them a clearer picture of how your company benefits their business. And close again for the meeting. If even your mom and dad call you and they are starting a business tomorrow and want to use your services, you schedule an *appointment* to meet with them. Got it?

What happens if the suspect objects to the meeting? You have to be ready for this. Resistance is a natural part of the sales process, and you should be expecting it as such. In fact, the number one answer in sales is "no." If you are getting "no" a lot, you probably aren't doing much wrong. The difference maker in sales is how you handle the common objections people give you over the phone. Gehegan describes these objections as reflexive.

You're in a department store and you are shopping for a television. The sales associate approaches and asks if she can help you with something. Guess what you say instantly? "I'm just kind of browsing." What does the sales associate do? They do what most salespeople do; they give up too quickly handling objections. She tells you that if you need anything her name is Anne, and she'll be over in the shoe section.

Why do you say, "I'm just looking or I'm just browsing?" It's reflexive. Habitual. Instinctive. Business owners get dozens of phone calls and in-person visits from sales reps every week. They are very used to saying, "I'm good. I'm fine. I don't need anything." The better salespeople have learned to not give in and to nudge, not push them closer to the decision they want.

The general rule on the phone is to try and handle three objections from the decision maker before ending the call. You must have a clear and concise *response* to her objection and then quickly a *request for action*. Here's a common example: "I'm too busy to meet." Your response, "I can appreciate you working on a tight schedule. I would be glad to arrange an appointment at your convenience perhaps before 8:00 a.m. or after 6:00 p.m." Request for action, "Could we get together next Tuesday at 7:30 a.m.?" Many sales reps are pretty good coming up with a response, but shockingly, they forget to add the most critical component—the request for action.

Learning this technique and mastering what to say to some of the more common objections you face in your business will give you the confidence to obey the rule of handling three objections before you give up. The more times you follow the rule, the more appointments that were previously slipping through your hands will stay put. There is obviously one exception to the rule of handling three objections. If the objections are staying constant in their intensity or escalating in their intensity, then abandon the rule and professionally and politely end the call.

Of course, all the above applies to you speaking with the decision maker. It all becomes pointless if you can't get through to the decision maker. Your success navigating the gatekeeper or frontline receiver of the phone call at the business determines your success with the decision maker. I've read lots of books and pieces on gatekeeper techniques, and most all have salient points, but nothing compares to John Gehegan's approach.

Two fundamental things have to be in place the second the gatekeeper answers the phone. They are an attitude of expectation and an attitude of assumption. The expectation is handled by what you say. The assumption is handled by how you say it. First, the expectation. What do you signal to the gatekeeper, either consciously or subconsciously, when you say things like, "Is he available? Is she in? I was wondering if I could speak to him?" Mainly, you're giving away that the call is unexpected. If the call were expected, why would you have to ask if she is in?

What do gatekeepers do with unexpected phone calls? Screen them! What do they do with expected calls? They put them through without asking you a single question. Therefore, the opening line is, "This is [your name] *calling* for [her name]." The "calling for" gives the inference that the call may well be expected. Notice, no company name is mentioned. Why?

Let's say you work for an insurance company, and you say, "This is Jack with ABC Insurance, and I wanted to talk to Ms. Decision Maker." The gatekeeper hears ABC Insurance, not Jack. He quickly deduces that they already use DEF Insurance. What happens? You guessed it. He proceeds to tell you that they already have a provider in place, and Ms. Decision Maker doesn't need or want to speak to you. Eliminate potential roadblocks.

Next is the assumption component. How you say it matters. Notice the above opening line ends with a period. So say the sentence the same way you say any statement. Read the following sentence: "Put the book on the table." Did you hear how you said it? Now read this sentence: "Put the book on the table?" Notice a difference? Your voice typically trails up when a sentence ends with a question mark. It trails down when it ends with a period.

I'm here to tell you, if your voice trails up in its pitch when you say the opening line to the gatekeeper, you're going to trigger a primal reaction for the gatekeeper to ask more questions for clarification. Let the screening begin. It is amazing that something so seemingly simple can be dramatic in improving how the gatekeeper reacts to you. In your voice, be assumptive and confident. Not arrogant or obnoxious, but comfortable and assured.

Lastly, remember the rule of three when handling the objections with the decision maker? That rule does not apply to the gatekeeper. Mainly because if you stop and think about it, the gatekeeper never gives you *objections*! He or she mainly asks you *questions*! "Is she expecting your call?" "Does he know what this is about?" "What company are you with?" "What is this regarding?" Not a single objection in the lot. If a gatekeeper were giving you *objections*, it might sound like this: "She doesn't take unsolicited calls." "He wouldn't be interested in that." "She's too busy to schedule appointments." Regardless, hang in there until the gatekeeper relents and lets you through! You still want to use the respond-and-request-action approach to the gatekeeper's questions. Be professional. Be polite. Be persistent. The goal with the gatekeeper is simple: it is to get to the decision maker.

The final thought on this critical part of the universe, outbound calling, is not to take the rejection personally. Many salespeople neglect calling on the phone for fear of running into the rude person or getting hung up on. The substantial amount of people you call on the phone are going to be pleasant, even if they don't want or need what you are trying to sell. There are few in number who are just plain rude. Why sacrifice the many potential "yeses" for the limited rude "nos?"

In over thirty years of making calls myself or coaching others on calls, I've learned a couple of things about "rude" people. First, they are more quicker getting out of the way and getting you one step closer to your next "yes." I would rather have the decision maker tell me to get lost in ten seconds, than the one who tells me each month he's closer to making a decision, and ten months later, I have the same thing from both of them: nothing. At least I know where I stand with the rude one—the other one I'm hoping every month that this is the month.

I have probably counted on him to help me reach or surpass my goal month after month. All he does is continue to "think it over" week after week. Can I let you in on a little secret? The one taking forever isn't sold. A very wise person once taught me that the buyer is uncontrollable, only your activity is controllable. So give me the rude guy! And maybe I should cut my bait on the other one while I'm at it.

Second, I've learned that rude people who talk to you that way when they don't know you often talk to you worse when they know you. Be honest. Can you think of someone in your portfolio or book of business right now you wish would leave? That's this guy! You know, always has a problem? Always trying to call your boss and her boss? Luckily for you, enhanced activity eliminates all this. So embrace the rude Randys; they're actually helping you out!

Finally, what do we do about hang-ups. Let me give you a four-letter word you are actually able to use in public: next! Someone who does not give someone a few seconds of common decency on the phone? Next! Is that the kind of client you want to add to your book? Now hear this, I do try to give someone the benefit of the doubt. We have all had "bad" days—maybe a little short with people from time to time—so I try to take that into consideration. I may try that decision maker back in a week or so. If it happens again, there's the pattern. He's done.

Next!

Chapter 3

The Prospecting Principle

Allan Congrave is a close friend. He was the best man in my wedding. He is English, and with all due respect to the Queen, he is a crazy Brit! His sense of humor is unmatched, and his wit is razor sharp. Although I tease him often of his loyalty to Liverpool and that *real* football is the Dallas Cowboys vs. the Pittsburgh Steelers, he is one of the best sales representatives and sales managers I have ever worked with.

After a very successful stint in sales covering the Dallas, Texas market for the company we both worked for, he was promoted to become the sales manager in Houston, Texas. The company we worked for was TeleCheck. TeleCheck was a company and now a system that helped merchants safely accept checks at the point of sale. Once a check was approved by TeleCheck, the merchant could safely accept the check for the purchase of goods or services. If the check bounced or could not come to fruition, TeleCheck would cover the check. The merchants were guaranteed their money.

Over 1,200 sales representatives would sell this service to merchants all over the US and abroad. Over the evolution of the check, our reps began to sell a variety of merchant services including credit card, point-of-sale equipment, electronic check acceptance, and even systems for banks to safely accept new clients as checking and saving account holders. Because of the unique services we provided, our representatives had no choice but to go out and be pure hunters for new business. There weren't many banks or other partners in the early days providing tons of leads. We had to go out and sell who we were *and* what we did.

When Allan was promoted to become the sales manager of the Houston sales team, it was a big deal in lots of ways. One of the biggest was his sales team was also based in the corporate offices of TeleCheck. If any team needed to perform well, it would have to be the Houston team. The benefit was, at any time, Allan could go up a few floors of the building and get scoop on all the newest and latest things TeleCheck was doing. His team would always be the test group for new ideas, new services, and new products. But also, the CEO could go down a few floors, walk into his office, and wonder what in the world was going on? The position was prestigious in some ways and more stressful some too. If anyone was built to handle this perfectly, it was a limey with a quick wit, an even temper, and a professional who could get things done.

One day, Allan decided to do a sales blitz with his team. His sales force at the time was made up of about fifteen salespeople who covered the greater Houston market. As many a manager often does, every now and then, he does a little competitive blitz to energize his team. His idea was to have his team work in pairs and blanket the market over the course of a day. He had all sorts of goals and prizes for various parts of the blitz, but the main focus was on cold calling new business prospects. He had a few new salespeople on the team and felt this would help them gain more confidence and success paired up with some of his seasoned vets.

A few days before the blitz, he called me in my office a few floors above his and asked me if I was in town, would I be available to help out? He had an odd number and needed me to pair up with one of his salespeople. I told him I would be happy to help.

On the day of the blitz, we were to be there at 7:30 a.m. Allan addressed his team and did the normal explanations of the event. We were to be back at 4:30 p.m. to share our results, award the winners, and enjoy some refreshments. Here I was, introduced to my partner, Rick.

Rick had only been on the job for two weeks. In fact, he had just finished all the necessary training. I guessed he was probably twenty-two or twenty-three years old. Nice kid. He seemed quiet and reserved, which would have been expected for both being so new to the team and probably starting his first “real” job after college.

It didn't help matters that he was paired with the corporate trainer for the blitz. On our walk to the garage and once in the car, we engaged in the normal conversations that one who had been with the company a long time and one brand-new would have. Our territory to blitz was already predetermined by Allan, and it was a good one. The area was rich with store fronts, industrial parks, and more.

When we found our place to start, I told him that I would do the first few, and then he could take a few and rotate it like that for the day. He then looked at me and said that he hated cold calling. He said he was terrified of walking in on complete strangers. My first thought was, *Are you kidding me?* I tried to reconcile his newness to his nerves, but he went on to make it very clear that he didn't want to do it. I assured him that he would survive, and that I would be right beside him no matter what the outcome of the call.

Honestly, I have been "thrown" out of places from Seattle to Manhattan many times, so it no longer bothered me. Some of the best experiences I had in sales were actually getting told to leave immediately. I learned quickly not to take it personally. They had no idea of anything about me nor what I had to offer. So why let that matter? They chose not to take advantage of something that was benefitting many of their business neighbors. It was their loss in my mind.

I used to visualize them having to deal with bad checks the very next day, not knowing that had they listened to what we could bring to the table, it could have eliminated the problem. I also learned the concept of "next." This one said "no," so see what the *next* one says. A perfect illustration of this is what happened one time in Chicago.

I am from Florida. I like sunshine, beaches, and heat. I'm not built for clouds, frozen lakes, and cold. It seemed like all the cold weather districts in TeleCheck called for my help during their coldest months. I'm sure that wasn't a provable fact, but it sure felt true.

I found myself cold calling with a rep in downtown Chicago, Illinois, in early January 1996. Literally, cold calling. In the hotel the night before, the local Chicago meteorologist was announcing that it would be the coldest weather in the city in thirty years. So here we were, downtown Chicago, coldest weather in thirty years, snow falling, and walking in on total strangers.

After a few calls, we walked into a business and instantly upon entering, a person we assumed to be the owner yelled across the room, "Whatever you're selling, we don't want it! Get out!" Being the corporate trainer, I had to not give up so easy in front of the rep, so I kept walking and began to say something like, "Well, sir, if you give us just a moment..." He cut me off very quick, and in his most stereotypical Chicago accent, told us to get out. The very *next* business we walked into, brushing the snow off our coats, the owner came out and asked us, "Are you out cold calling in this weather?" We said we were. He proceeded to say that anyone that dedicated was someone who deserved to be heard. He took us back to his office and listened to the pitch. True story.

My assurances to Ricky were not helping. I took the lead and walked in and out of businesses for a good hour. He just stood beside me, watching me work, not saying a word. I told him I thought it was time for him to dive in and give it a try. His face looked similar to one made right when the dentist tells you that "this might hurt a little bit." He froze and refused. He made excuses that he still wasn't ready yet. So I trudged on. I had a lot of other things I could have been doing in my office, but for Allan's sake, I forged onward.

We talked to a few people here and there. There was nothing of any magnitude happening, and then this kid asks if it was time for lunch? By this time, I had tried all the motivational and psychological tools. Nothing was working, and he wanted lunch. I told him that I would be happy to stop for lunch. It was time he learned about a prospecting lunch anyway. I found the nearest convenience store, bought two questionable chicken-salad sandwiches, two bottles of lemonade, and we had lunch in my car in the parking lot. Lunch was about fifteen minutes. We kept going.

I resigned myself that Ricky wasn't going to do anything. So I decided to go all out. We walked into dozens of more businesses. Around 4:00 p.m., we happened into a business that sold spas, hot tubs, and similar recreational equipment. The owner was there and welcomed our conversation. After a few minutes, we moved to his office. I went through the process of needs assessment and looking for that definite need.

After a very good discussion, he says, "It's ironic you guys came in today. I've been looking for a new provider, and I like what I hear. Let's do it." He had seven locations around town. He switched all his merchant services, added electronic check acceptance, and *leased* two new POS terminals for each location. It took me an hour to fill out all the paperwork! It was one of the best cold-call closes I had ever experienced. The commission on this deal for the rep was going to be large! And he hadn't done a thing.

Needless to say, we didn't make it back by 4:45 p.m. It was 6:00 p.m. Everyone had left. Blitz over. As always, Allan was still there working late. We came into his office and shared with him this huge deal. Allan was thrilled. The revenue this new client would produce would be very beneficial. All was well. Then Ricky left, and I stayed in Allan's office.

As soon as the coast was clear, I told him about our day and how this guy was afraid to walk through a door and much less open his mouth. Allan said that Ricky was very confident through the interview process and presented himself as a go-getter. I told him that he might have a problem on his hands. He thanked me for helping out, closing the deal, and I left.

The next morning, I get a call from Allan, and he asked me to come down to his office. When I got down there, he asked me to walk with him over to Ricky's desk. On it were his badge, his demo equipment, all his company manuals and work products, and a note. The note read: "I'm very sorry, but this isn't the job for me." Too bad for him. His commission on the deal was worth close to $7,000. to $10,000.

Prospecting Principle

So what is my prospecting principle? Whatever sales position you have or position you're going to explore, remember that *A*ctivity *C*reates *T*riumphs. You have to be *ACT*ive. You must be pro*ACT*ive. You must always keep your *ACT*ivity going. Do you know the number one reason salespeople are let go from any organization? Would you guess it's because they're not smart enough? Do you think it's because they're not trained enough? Is it because they're not talented enough? Is it because their pricing is not competitive enough or products aren't superior to the competition? Wrong, wrong, wrong, and doubly wrong.

An easy answer is that they are not hitting their goals or quotas. Aha, you're on to something. But that is *act*ually the symptom of the problem. The reason is quite simple: they did not do enough *act*ivity to get in front of enough people, to get the necessary ones to do what they needed them to do. Think about your results from last month for a moment. If you exceeded your goals, good for you. But think about how you got there. What portion were leads or unsolicited referrals? Was it one or two big deals that pushed you over the top?

If so, you're walking a thin line. I have seen many a sales rep working that big deal, praying it comes through. It's a great stall for their manager. "It's coming! It's coming!" "This might be the month." "When it hits, it's going to be great for everyone!" And when it does, this is true. And when it doesn't? I could go through endless clichés, like putting all your eggs in one basket, but *even* the month that it hits, why are you relying on just that? As a sales and district manager, I have had to let several salespeople go because that "big deal" never came through.

What if you didn't exceed your goals last month? Think about how you *didn't* get there. Weed through a lot of the easy excuses like the ones I mentioned above, and I think you will find the prospecting principle staring you in the face: *A*ctivity *C*reates *T*riumphs. Also, *A*ctivity *C*ompensates for *T*rials. How was your *act*ivity in the two months *prior* to the month you fell short? What you do "today" does not bear fruit "today." Who plants a tomato plant in the morning and expects a ripe tomato that evening? Who plants one seed and expects a garden? *ACT*ivity is your best friend in sales. The more time spent with your best friend, the better the relationship.

If you have spent any time in sales or have read other sales books, you've heard of something like the "sales funnel." I could sit here and try to come up with a better analogy, but sometimes, the original thought can't be improved. For example, oxygen was a pretty good original thought. Hard to improve on that. Imagine a funnel. What you put through the funnel comes out the bottom of the funnel.

So in the perfect utopian sales funnel, all the suspects move through the funnel, turn into prospects, and fall out the end as new happy clients. Welcome to Fantasy Land! What *act*ually happens is you put a few suspects in the funnel, and you try to turn some of them into *act*ual prospects. This is the middle of the funnel. This is where you make your money. This is where you spend a lot of time.

You can't turn some of these to clients because of things like not able to negotiate terms, loss to competition, lack of inertia, and not able to approve. So you're spending much of your time here, and you should; this is where you make the results and money you'd like to earn. Eventually, you get some of them to close; they become clients and leave the funnel. Good job. Question: While spending a lot of time in the middle of the funnel, were you still spending the necessary time feeding the funnel? It is not the easiest thing to do. I have seen many reps have huge months. Killed it! Guess which month was their worst? The answer is the one right after their busiest.

Good *ACT*ivity solves the majority of your sales problems. Earlier we revealed the areas of the universe at your disposal. Make sure you plan your month around your *act*ivity. Every month with no exception must be focused on *act*ivity *first*. Remember your *act*ivity that you're planning for in the *current* month is for the results in *future* months. Don't let the temptation to put it off because of how busy you are closing business now and let it affect the results you will need later.

Block specific times within the weeks of your month solely dedicated to your prospecting *act*ivity. I know of a very successful rep who used to do full prospecting days on Mondays and Fridays of every week. She didn't buy into the false myth that decision makers didn't meet with people on those days. Out of 1,200-plus salespeople across the country, she was in the top 10 five years in a row.

Have you encountered the prospect who keeps putting you off? She makes you believe that she is coming to a decision soon? Do you have the one that tells you they need to think it over, and their thinking-it-over process drags on forever? My guess would be she isn't sold in the first place, and we will discuss that in later chapters. In the meantime, remember this: the buyer is uncontrollable, only your *act*ivity is.

The more people who you can put into that funnel, the greater the chances you will find the ones to make you your success. I don't know where Ricky is today. I'm sure he found what he excels at and hope is doing well. At least for him, he quickly decided that he wasn't cut out to do what it would take to make it in this kind of sales situation. He simply didn't want to do the *act*ivity. Do you? Get your *ACT* together and in good order, and the stress that comes trying to hit goals and quotas in your sales position will prominently subside.

Chapter 4

The Opening of Any Call

I love football. College football, professional football, arena league football, high school football; if there is a football involved, I'm glued to it. My dad introduced it to me when I was a kid. We lived just outside of the Orlando, Florida area in the early seventies and back then we didn't have any real local sports teams to cheer for. Sadly, not too much has changed in forty-five years because the only major professional sports team is the Orlando Magic. No football, no baseball, no nothing.

So in a time that many of you reading this book can't remember, there were only three network TV stations. There was no such thing as cable TV or satellite TV. So whatever came on channels 2, 6, or 9 was what we watched. So naturally, I gravitated to the teams that always seemed to be on national TV.

The Dallas Cowboys won my heart even though the Pittsburgh Steelers kept beating them in the Super Bowl. The Los Angeles Dodgers and New York Yankees were seemingly always in the World Series. I chose to like the Dodgers because their blue was cooler than the Yankees' blue. Not too much longer, the Boston Celtics and Los Angeles Lakers were always on with Magic and Bird going at it. I figured I'd side with the Celtics since they were closer geographically than the Lakers. Funny, I didn't use that logic with the Yankees.

Of all the sports, football was my favorite. I can't explain it, but I just love how the concept of grown men trying to move a ball, sometimes only one yard, fascinated me. One time, I pulled out a yardstick and placed it on the ground. And I would look back at the

TV and wonder what was so difficult in moving forward three little feet. It seemed so easy.

The rules in football change over time, and in the old days, whichever team won the coin toss would choose to either kick off or receive the football. Even the coin toss was exciting because every team wanted to win it so they could get the ball first and try to make a statement. Very rarely, a team would choose to kick off, and even that I found fascinating. Why would you let the other team have the ball? What if they drove it right down and scored a quick touchdown? Now your psyche is damaged, you're behind, and neither of those situations is good. You want the ball! You want to go first. You want to put the pressure on the other team.

Well, a few years back, they changed even the rule of the coin toss—that if the team won it, they could defer. What? In other words, it goes like this: "Hey, Dallas, you won the toss. What would you like to do?" Dallas then says that they really don't care or they can't make up their mind so they'll give it back to the other team to decide. What? You almost don't need a coin toss. At first glance, it seemed dumb to me. But now it makes all the sense in the world.

When the team defers, it speaks confidence, not cowardice. They are saying to go ahead and try to score on us. We're going to stop you. And the team that defers gets the ball to start the ever-important second half too. What does any of this have to do with the sales call? Well, the opening of the call is very much like the coin toss at a football game. And from now on, the first thing you need to do is learn how to defer.

As mentioned in the foreword of this book, John J. Gehegan has been the singular inspiration and motivating figure for my sales success. I have spent many an hour on phone call appointments and face-to-face appointments with him. Early on, I would say, "So how are we going to start off?" He would explain that we weren't going to start off; they were going to start off. In essence, he was going to defer to them right off the bat.

I must admit it sounded and, during the first few times, felt awkward. But what did I know? I thought that the minute someone agreed to an appointment, it meant he was ready to sit down and hear all about my products and services. As soon as the appointment commenced, I was to give the history of my company, who they were, who I was, what we have, and how he gets it!

Well, I have now learned, in many years, that approach seldom works. The buyer has to already be in definite need for that to be effective. I will get into the subject of indefinite need and definite need soon, but for now, definite need is the catalyst for buying something. We, salespeople, have to develop definite need with the majority of the people we meet with, but sometimes, the prospect is already there. For example, when a prospect contacts you directly. I have a leak under my sink. Water is flowing into the kitchen. I need a plumber. I call the plumber. The plumber doesn't have to do a lot of convincing to whether or not I will use his services. Furthermore, I will probably pay his rate with little resistance.

So how should this all work on the initial appointment with a prospect and this strategy of the defer? First, we must make sure we've done our homework before the appointment to insure as much success as possible. I am assuming that you've already done your assessment of the possible prospect before booking the appointment in the first place. Not everyone outside your office is a prospect for you. So this appointment should be with a specifically targeted business with which you would like to partner. To the best of your knowledge and ability, the appointment is with the appropriate decision maker for what you offer. You've probably spent time researching a bit about the industry to learn trends, competitors, and other things that will help you sound informed during the meeting. Now we need to focus on how the actual appointment is going to unfold.

To this day, when John and I are having a major call with a prospective or existing client; we get together a half hour before the appointment to discuss where we want to go with this call. What is the objective? What are the next steps? With he in San Diego and I in Orlando, this works best for us. Now don't get me wrong; we talk about upcoming appointments throughout our weeks and months leading up to it; we don't just "show up" ten minutes before and "figure it out."

Even so, we always convene together a few minutes before and discuss who is going to lead certain areas, and to quote John,

"Where we want to go with this." If our appointments are in person, and we've flown out to some city in America, then we spend time together doing the same diligence. John has a really sharp sales mind, and through watching him work, I've learned some clear objectives on these calls. It's pretty easy to figure out what mine were, but I learned to start thinking as much or more on what my prospect's objectives might be. Honestly, I hadn't really given it much thought in the early part of my career in sales.

Your Objectives

You have five main objectives in any initial appointment with a prospective client:

- ✓ Introduce yourself and your company's approach
- ✓ Establish rapport
- ✓ Gain an understanding of the prospect's process where your company applies
- ✓ Probe for definite need
- ✓ Advance the process with a specific next step

Prospect's Objectives

Your prospect has five main objectives during the initial appointment with a sales person:

- ✓ Learn about your company's approach
- ✓ Learn about you
- ✓ Evaluate your alternatives
- ✓ See if it makes economic sense
- ✓ Determine what's in it for him or her

So your objectives can be summarized this way. In meeting with this decision maker, what is her current methodology, what are the strengths and weaknesses of the current methodology, and how is a decision made? Your prospect's objectives can be summarized this way. In meeting with this sales person, does she have something that can improve, strengthen, or streamline my business and its effect on my customers for a reasonable cost to buy it?

After the early pleasantries are exchanged in the meeting, you should have an opening benefit statement. I would encourage you to use the same one each time. It becomes part of your sales DNA. The statement should contain three parts: 1) introduces your company; 2) establishes capability; and 3) provides an agenda. This statement should be brief! I've heard many reps start by saying things like, "The company started in 1958 by two guys and a horse and…" Yikes! Stop it! The prospect is already watching the clock! Try something like this:

> *We have helped our clients maximize cash flow by optimizing the speed at checkout. We offer a variety of products and services each of which can be tailored to meet your specific needs. My objective today is to learn about how your checkout process currently works and determine if we can offer you some cost-saving alternatives.*

After the opening benefit statement is done, a lot of salespeople just keep on going and going, and the presentation becomes a monologue instead of a dialogue. Others spend so much time building "rapport" that by the time they get to the meat of why they were there, there is no time. Give your opening benefit statement and then guess what? Defer.

The defer is most effective when the prospect has received initial information in their contact with you. For example, I have spent the last sixteen-plus years calling on banks. I go back and forth with the executive's administrative assistant or even the executive directly. I have forwarded an email with a link to our website or an attachment of digital collateral with my brief request for a phone appointment. This gets to the decision maker, and I get the appointment scheduled. Maybe I have direct mailed and sent a packet of information to the prospective decision maker. Regardless of the method, he or she has some information and overviews of what we do. I have a scheduled appointment, and I have just finished my excellent opening benefit statement. Now defer to them.

John Gehegan does this so adeptly. He is so matter-of-fact and assumptive I look forward to hearing it. It's fun sitting there knowing it's coming. He does a great opening benefit statement and then immediately sends it back over to the decision maker. It normally comes out something like this, "So, Roger, I'd like to throw it back to you and see from what we've sent you and briefly talked about what questions you might have about what we do and our process?" Bam. We haven't been in the meeting or on the call for more than three minutes.

So what does this quick defer do? Well, there are numerous benefits but let me highlight a few. First, it instantly engages the decision maker. He or she quickly realizes that the involvement level is instant. This isn't going to be a twenty-minute presentation/monologue with questions at the end. Decision makers get lots of those. Not this time; you want them involved and involved early.

Second, it certainly sheds a little light on their real interest level. Let's face it; we have all been on sales appointments where the owner didn't half remember it, you, or what it was for. She probably agreed to the appointment because she was having an amazing day and all the answers were "yes" that day. Then appointment time comes around and either you get a no-show or a cursory meeting that goes very quickly.

If you have sent information, materials, or other collateral pre-appointment, a decision maker who has a vested interest in the appointment will have looked through them and have questions. So when you defer, you can instantly tell. I have sat with John in person and many calls, where it was obvious the other person hadn't done much homework before our meeting.

And their stumbling responses or vague questions were sometimes both uncomfortable and humorous. Funny how if *you* were the one unprepared, they would quickly determine you might not be someone they want to work with. Luckily, the previous example hasn't happened all that much.

Most of the people that we have had serious dialogue with had done their due diligence. They had looked over what was sent and had some very good and interesting questions, which leads me to my last highlight. Third, their questions tend to point to where the need lies, how we might compare to something already in place, and where their mindset might be.

The deeper the questions, the more they've thought about it and given you the fairness of a meaningful meeting—the quicker they are engaged in the meeting, and the signal that the door could possibly be open—for them to become your next client.

Get the prospect or client involved early. You're basically asking her, "Why did you agree to this meeting?" You will then begin to gauge pretty quickly if you've got something of some substance or not. Then you can navigate more adeptly how to work the meeting to your advantage.

Chapter 5

The Two Reasons People Buy Anything

Los Angeles, California, is an interesting place. The weather is spectacular. The ocean is spied on by wonderful cliffs and mountains out in the distance. Maybe you run into a movie star, or see a TV show as part of a live audience. Any cuisine you crave, LA has it.

Like sports? Well, some of the most famous and successful sports teams are sprinkled all over the city. Shopping, you wonder? Stroll down Melrose Avenue or Rodeo Drive.

Do you hate traffic? The price you pay for all the fun is mitigated most of the time by the horrible traffic.

In LA's defense, she is the second largest city in America, but the traffic in and around town can be discouraging. When I would work with our Los Angeles sales reps, the running joke was that you never say to a potential prospect, "I'll meet with you Tuesday morning at 9:00 a.m." It was always, "I'll meet with you between 9:00 a.m. and 10:00 a.m. on Tuesday morning." In Los Angeles, the six-mile trip that only took you fifteen minutes yesterday would take you forty-five minutes at the same exact time the next day and for no apparent reason. Whatever traffic you think you deal with, it doesn't compare to that of Los Angeles. (That is unless you work and live in the Tysons Corner, Virginia, area. You're the only exception.)

I enjoyed working with our Los Angeles sales reps. They all embodied the "LA vibe." They were both laid back yet very competitive. It was here that I met Brian. He was brand-new the first time I worked with him. He was with the company maybe two months. He had been there long enough to get through some training and to have a few experiences out in the field. I always enjoyed working with the newer reps. Their eagerness to learn was strong. They actually listened to what I said, and they hadn't already developed many "bad habits." Brian was no different, he was a sharp kid; and he had the willingness to learn and the desire to be successful. My kind of sales rep!

It came time for me to work with Brian one-on-one out in the field. We met early, which, in Los Angeles, is 9:00 a.m. Thankfully, he had two appointments. One was mid-morning and the other was mid-afternoon. As I now try to remember back, I can't tell you what the first appointment was. Clearly, it was nondescript. The main reason I can't recall that first appointment is because the second meeting is the one I will never forget. The story is not only for an analogy for the focus of this chapter, but the appointment had also come in as a lead. It was also because it was funny, at least to me.

We met the owner for the afternoon meeting. He was a very nice man. He owned about four fairly large tire stores located around the greater Los Angeles area. We met with him in a large warehouse where he kept his office. It was full of more tires in one place I have ever seen before or sense. Since Brian was fairly new, he had reasonable apprehension for the meeting, so I told him not to worry and that I would take the lead.

The meeting couldn't have gone any easier. After a brief exchange (I hadn't learned how to defer yet), I began to ask him a few questions to see if there might be a need for him to utilize what we were offering. Not soon after, he stops me and says that one of his business buddies who owns a few auto shops was telling him about our service. He used it in all his shops and loved it. Our potential prospect was already having issues with his current provider and got our information from his peer and called for someone to come out and see him. His pal practically sold him for us and gave him lots of information.

He said, "If Rooney recommends it, then it must be the real deal. Sign me up. I'm cancelling the other service and want you guys as soon as possible." I looked over to Brian and asked him to get the contracts out from his briefcase. The gentleman and I continued talking. He was not happy about this provider. He wanted their equipment gone, and he wanted ours. He wanted the same setup as Rooney. After a minute, I looked back over to Brian. He was busy pulling out our point-of-sale equipment demo and leaning down for a place to plug it in. No contracts had been retrieved.

In the heat of the moment, I moved my leg over and "kicked" his leg. Trying to say, "What are you doing?" "Stop what you're doing!" "Put that away and get the contracts" all the while continuing my conversation with the owner! It was like a scene from Laurel and Hardy! Luckily, the prospect couldn't see the shenanigans happening on our side of the desk.

You see, Brian was trying to follow what he had learned in his training. He was trained that you now show the demonstration of the equipment. However, the owner was quite clear that he was ready to change. He already had reached the point of what he felt he needed, and he didn't care what the equipment was.

What would have happened if Brian had botched the demo? What would have happened if there was some sort of problem with the equipment, and it failed to properly demonstrate what it was designed to do? Then what would we have done? The good news is, Brian would probably have done a great demo and the chances of the equipment malfunctioning was nil. That wasn't the point. The buyer had already made it clear he wasn't happy with what he had; he knew Rooney was doing great and had gotten the recommendation to switch already. At this moment, all we needed to do was sign the contract. The owner wasn't going to be dealing with the point-of-sale equipment anyway; that was up to his staff to use it. So, Brian, get the contracts out, and let's sign up this brand-new client!

There are two reasons people buy anything. Whether someone is buying shoes, cars, Big Macs, insurance, you name it, they only do so when two conditions are met. 1) They see the need or the problem; and 2) they want to do something about it. Many sales reps are pretty skilled at part 1: getting prospects or clients to see the need. Where they fail the most is getting to part 2: getting them to want to do something about it.

The technical sales terminology is indefinite need vs. definite need. Indefinite need is best described as what the sales person "sees," and definite need is what the prospect or client "sees." All of us salespeople are guilty of sometimes thinking we know the problem, and we obviously know that we have the solution. It doesn't matter if the decision maker doesn't see it or agree; it's a problem that needs to be solved!

I can remember early on as a merchant sales representative walking into a possible new client's business and noticing an old point-of-sale terminal near the cash register. Immediately, I thought that was a problem. Why are they using such a terminal? The one I have is newer and better and has lots more shiny buttons. Surely, he would love to switch to mine! I was ready to sell. Well, *after* my stellar ten-minute demonstration on my newer equipment, I sadly learned that he didn't even accept checks and only took in about three or four credit cards a month! Why would he drop $700 on a new terminal? The one he had was doing just fine for what he *needed.*

Many salespeople sell to *indefinite need.* Those same salespeople are walking out the door, scratching their head, wondering what went wrong? Success in sales happens when you learn that people buy something when they move to *definite need.* I learned early on, and fairly quickly, to not jump the gun when I noticed, or even as I heard something, the prospect had or did that I thought I could immediately fix or improve.

I must say, it is a hard thing to fight off. Your instincts can be strong and sometimes right, but the danger of losing it outweighs the minimal success of getting it. So first, we have to recognize that what we think they need (indefinite need) needs to be moved to where they agree that there is a need (definite need.)

If you are a sales person who actually walks into businesses, take a good look around, especially for the things that may enhance your case for getting the prospect to want to make a change to you. If you are selling over the phone or by other means, listen to what is being told to you from the gatekeeper all the way to the decision maker. They may drop bits of information that strengthens your pitch when the time is right. Now there is no doubt that a newer product or a faster and more convenient service would absolutely enhance and improve the overall productivity of the business. I mean, you have hundreds of clients that have already taken advantage of it, right?

The skill is to work your way to making it a definite need. Imagine you are sitting on a chair, reading a book. Your prospect is sitting on the couch across from you. You're reading the story. You see the words. You understand what's happening. The goal is to get that prospect to figuratively come over to you and look over your shoulder and *see* what you're reading and *see* the story themselves. I guess that's where the old expression "let's get on the same page" comes from.

As I mentioned, most salespeople are okay with helping the decision maker to identify a possible need. The hardest part, in my opinion, is getting the decision maker to want to do something about it. The second of the two reasons people buy is not easy. Another good way to define that second reason is creating a sense of urgency. Many prospects or clients may wholeheartedly agree that there is a problem. They see it clearly. It probably needs to be addressed. But they also feel "it isn't ***that*** big of a problem." "It doesn't really need to be addressed right now." "There's other ways to work around it." This can be extremely frustrating!

How many times have you been in the meeting feeling great! This is going awesome. Here we go! Only for the decision maker to say something like, "This all looks good. Give me some time to think through it and call me back in a couple of weeks or months, and we'll go from there." What just happened? It was all so perfect. Well, the problem is, the person needs to see the problem *and* want to do something about it. In other words, the sense of urgency is attached.

Let me give you an example that illustrates the sense of urgency impact. I could be in a meeting seated comfortably in my chair, and one of my fellow associates could notice that I have a hole in the bottom of one of my shoes. He could approach me and say, "Hey! You have a hole in the sole of your shoe. You should probably get that fixed. My sister is the manager of a shoe store here in town, and I can make sure she gives you a discount on a new pair of shoes! Want her name and contact information?"

Well, I could take a look at the hole and determine that it really isn't that big of a hole. It doesn't really bother me because I only wear these shoes every other day. Next time, I'll keep my feet on the ground so no one sees it! Even with a nice discount, I'm not wearing them enough to justify buying a new pair of shoes. There's no real sense of urgency, even with the promise of a price decrease.

However, I could look at the hole in the bottom of my shoe and realize that I wear these shoes a lot. In fact, I do my best cold calling in these shoes. I sure do spend a lot of time in parking lots, industrial sites, and construction sites; it rains a lot in Orlando and that hole sure could contribute to wet dirty sock—not to mention glass, nails, and lots of other things I would not want to step on or *in*! Why don't I get that contact information? I just might need a new pair sooner rather than later? The sense of urgency in that scenario is certainly increased.

If you have conducted the meeting correctly, both of these components are in place, and that is when the decision maker moves forward with signing up for your product or services or giving you the necessary next steps to move the process forward. You see, at the outset, the person you are in front of is not a prospect until this happens. The actual sales term that she is at this moment is a suspect. I've been surprised over the years of how many salespeople, both new to sales or those that have been doing it a long time, do not recognize the difference between suspects and prospects.

A decision maker, when contacted out of the blue for the first time for an appointment, is a suspect. Now I do not mean the *criminal* definition of the word. I mean the *unknown* definition of the word. You don't know yet if the person wants or needs the product or service you're offering. You don't even know if you can give him the product or service you have yet. This is what the meeting is for, to see if he wants and you can supply the product or service to satisfy the need. Therefore, he is a suspect.

Your only goal dealing with suspects is to get the appointment. You don't tell your suspects about products, pricing, fees, benefits, and value when trying to schedule that appointment. That is reserved for potential prospects at the appointment. Remember, you don't even know if he needs it, or if you are able to supply it yet. So what is the definition of the noun “prospect”?

I ask this very question in all my business development classes. The majority of seasoned salespeople can’t answer the question correctly, at least in its entirety. Do you know the answer? If you said something like, “A potential client.” Well, you just joined about 85 percent of what everybody says. If you said something like, “Someone who wants to work with me, and I would like to work with her,” then you are with about 97 percent of what everybody says. Although these answers are on the right track, the answer isn’t fully complete.

A prospect has *three* components: 1) he or she has decided that they might want to work with you; 2) you have decided that you might be able to work with them; and 3) there is a specific next step set up to move the process forward. When those three components are met, you now have a prospect; any time *before* that, you have a suspect. Salespeople often neglect the third component, and this is where many of the delays and extension of the sales cycle happen. This moment happens at the very end of the meeting, and salespeople either use the technique of continuation or advancement. Guess which one is the weaker? Continuation. Guess which technique most salespeople choose? Continuation.

Is there such a thing as sales psychiatrist? I can’t even count the number of salespeople I have worked with tell me that during the end of a meeting, they begin to feel like they’ve taken too much of the decision maker’s time, and they need to quickly wrap up the meeting. What they actually do is change the letters of the word *wrap* and end up “warping” the meeting. They even feel like they don’t want to seem to push or ask for things, like referrals, because it’s all too much too soon.

I would hope that a sales psychiatrist would counsel them to see that this is all wrong! That’s why people use continuation. It’s easier, less intrusive and time-consuming. They come to the end of the meeting and say something like, “Well, Ms. Decision Maker, thanks for the time today. I’ll call you in a few days after you’ve had some time to digest and see where we need to go from here,” or “Hey, if you could get those financials (or statements, etc.) together that we talked about, I can touch base with you and work on getting them, and then we will work out what happens next." Then they get up and thank her for her time and leave. Guess what the sales person has right now? If you said nothing, you would be correct. You also just extended your sales cycle a significant number of days or weeks. All of that, not good.

Continuation is easier, less "pressure," weak, and less successful. The technique needed to employ is advancement. Advancement is best described as a *specific* next step set up to move the process forward. An example of advancement would go something like this, "Well, Ms. Decision Maker, thanks for the time today. As we talked about, I will need those financials we discussed to get the process moving forward. Am I able to pick those up, say, Monday afternoon around 3:00 p.m.?" Or "I really appreciate the things we've covered today through the meeting. Should we move forward with signing an agreement?" One of the best things I've learned to increase my success and shorten my sales cycle is to master using advancement over continuation.

Once you have these three things together: 1) someone willing to buy; 2) someone you might can sell; and 3) a specific next step, you now have a prospect. If you help that person see that there is a problem or need *and* get that person to move to a sense of urgency to do something about it, you have your next client. Remember this, *many* salespeople sell to the indefinite need; *all* people buy to the definite need. The definite need is reached when your prospects see the need and want to do something about it. I'll leave it at this. Your job is to get the prospect to see what you see, *or* for you to find out about things the prospect may not see yet!

Chapter 6

The One in Control

One of my favorite TV shows over the years was one called *The Practice.* It focused on a small defense firm, Robert Donnell and Associates. The lawyers were Bobby Donnell, Elleanor Frutt, Eugene Young, Lindsay Dole, and Jimmy Berluti. With a few exceptions, each episode tackled a certain case where the lawyers tried to defend some of the most horrendous clients. A few turned out to be innocent, but the majority were clearly guilty. Torn between their moral compasses and their ethical duties, it was riveting TV. At least to me. I recently found it available on one of the streaming sites and have started binge-watching it again. It still holds up, even after all these years.

Most all of the episodes take place in the courtroom—judge and jury present. Opposing district attorneys present. Courtroom gallery packed. My interest in the show was centered around the questioning of every witness by both the prosecutors and the defense. I couldn't get enough of how they prepped their witnesses for trial and determining the path they were going to take through their questions to present the best argument for their respective sides, then to see the actual testimony take place in the courtroom where many times it went pretty much as planned, but also several times it went off the rails.

It crossed my mind numerous times that it seemed that the lawyers or prosecutors were in complete control and, like an artist's rendering, painted the perfect picture of what had happened—only for the opposing side to come back and paint another picture of how it didn't. When both sides were on their game, it made for especially tense moments when the jury would come back to deliver its verdict. Oh, it was great. Many times I was shocked with the outcome.

Who is in control of a conversation: the one asking the questions or the one answering the questions? Well, whatever response popped in your head just gave you the answer! The person asking the questions is in control. Many people disagree with this assertion. For example, when I am working with salespeople trying to help them be a little more effective with their outbound calling, I ask them if they think we should ask the decision maker when she answers the phone, "Did I catch you at bad time, or do you have a moment?"

A lot would say, "No way. That only gives her an out." They are not exactly wrong; the decision maker could come back and say, "No. I'm busy." Or worse, they could just immediately hang up. With that in mind, my job is always to try to train or teach people what happens 99 percent of the time, not what happens 1 percent of the time. When you get that 1 percent who just hangs up, the only thing you control is to pick up the phone and call the next suspect! Back to the control question; it still begs the question, Who is? Let me ask you, the one reading this book, where were you born? What was your first pet? Did you go to college? Which one? Why did you choose that college? Do you like swimming or bowling? Are you getting the picture? Are you sure?

Even in this medium, I bet you could hear your subconscious answering those written questions! So back to my previous scenario; the decision maker says, "No. I'm busy." What do you do to stay in control? Ask another question. "No worries, when would be a better time to call you back?" The more questions you can ask, the better your control of the outcome. Somewhere, Bobby Donnell would be proud.

Probably the number one mistake I have seen (and also done myself) salespeople make is during the initial meeting with a client or prospect. They try to give information before they get the necessary information. I would have to ask that sales psychiatrist why he thinks this happens. He might agree with my assessment that salespeople start the meeting with the solution before identifying the need or problem. They seem trained or programmed to start off with something I call the "pitch and plead."

After introductions, the representative begins to explain who he is, what he does, who he does it for, why the decision maker should want it, how much it costs, and then begins the pleading for the decision maker to take it. In other words, way one-sided. They certainly don't know or follow the example laid out in chapter 4 about deferring to the client or decision maker early on to get them engaged in the conversation. The meeting is not a monologue; it should be a dialogue.

Just like in *The Practice*, you want to ask good questions to lead your client to the desired outcome. When *you tell them* what they may need, it is a whole lot different than when you help *them tell you* what they need. The art of asking good questions is a critical component of either making it or breaking it in a sales presentation.

You probably remember back in your school days in language arts about two main types of questions: open-ended questions and closed-ended questions. Closed-ended questions are pretty easy to ask. The answers are almost always one or two words. We ask them in our normal conversations, probably 85 percent of the time:

"Do you want to eat out tonight?"
"Where do you want to go?"
"Want me to pick you up?"
"What time?"
"Okay, I'll see you then."

We're all pretty good with closed-ended questions. The unsung heroes are the open-ended questions. These types of questions take a little more thought when asking them. The answers are usually lengthy and more detailed.

So what if the above close-ended questions were changed to open-ended ones?

"How do you feel about eating out tonight?"
"What are some of the restaurants you would like to try?"

"How would you like to meet up?"
"How does 6:00 p.m. work for you?"
"Okay, I'll see you then."

Most salespeople, if they even ask questions during the meeting, ask lots of closed-ended questions. Due to the short answers they elicit, it forces the sales rep to continue the dialogue; and once they abandon any question asking at all, it turns into a monologue faster.

When a sales person does all the talking, he or she is in trouble. They quicker fall into that trap of starting to give all the information without getting the necessary information, and the meeting ends at an impasse. Remember my hole-in-the-shoe example? Now I am not suggesting that your presentation be full of open-ended questions because that too would be odd. You have to ask good close-ended questions because they are the fastest fact finders. However, becoming more adept at sprinkling in some good open-ended questions will glean more information from the decision maker.

The more information they give you, the better to identify if they can even become a prospect in the first place. The broad idea of asking questions has now been a little more defined by the two general types of open- and close-ended questions. Now let's drill it down a step farther to really enhance your success.

Your questions must skillfully create a path for the decision maker or client to realize that she has a need and wants to do something about it. Then she becomes a buyer! There are four main steps and four types of questions that can help you get there more often than not.

<u>The four types of questions are</u>

1) Condition questions
2) Challenge questions
3) Consequence questions
4) Change questions

The four steps are

1) What are the current conditions within the business?
2) What are any challenges that arise in those conditions?
3) What are the consequences of those challenges continuing to exist?
4) What are the changes that can bring new and positive conditions to the business?

So you now have the meeting. After a brief introduction of you and your decision maker and normal pleasantries, it's time to start weaving the path of trying to move your suspect to a viable prospect. You want to see if you and she can determine if there is a definite need for your products or services. Maybe you have already identified in preplanning, or through your observations of her business, some things that *you* think you might or could improve.

Remember, this is *indefinite need*. The goal is to get her to see and acknowledge the same and move her to a sense of urgency, where she will decide to purchase or acquire those products or services. That is *definite need*. Many salespeople think they are so good, polished, and effective in delving into a monologue about what *they* have observed and immediately move to how they can change this decision maker's situation to a more positive situation. They have a slick presentation and think they can "move" the person into buying what they have. It does happen. I've seen it done. I will tell you, it is extremely rare.

However, most of the times that I *have* witnessed it, it was more often during a meeting with an *existing* client. The owner already was familiar with the sales rep, trust had already been established, and the owner would heed the sales person's counsel. When the two participants are unknown, the task is significantly harder. The best way to produce results is to follow the four steps. Practice the steps until you have them down.

Before you start speaking, remember that the person asking the questions controls the conversation. Oh, and here's a little extra bit of advice. The one who is doing the most talking is the one buying. The one who is doing the least talking is the one selling. Got it? All right, let's walk through the steps and get you some more sales!

Condition Questions

These questions are designed to figure out what is happening within the business now.

Many condition questions are closed ended, but the more open-ended condition-finding questions you can ask, the better!

Samples

- How are they currently taking payments?
- How do they currently try to improve cash flow?
- What steps do they take now to reduce overhead financial waste?
- How do they process their customers before, during, and at checkout?
- What things are in place now to handle vendors?
- How is their accounts payable department run?
- Where do they order and store and track inventory?
- Who do they use for their banking and financing needs?

Of course, there are all sorts of different types of businesses and sales representatives that provide services to those specific ones. So your goal at the onset, because you are familiar with the industries you sell to, is to find out the current conditions of the business that relate to your services. What are the processes they implement now? No selling here. Gathering the facts first.

Let's say in your preparation or initial discovery that you already see an area that may support her changing and buying what you have. Instead of jumping right into it, ask a few *condition questions* around that area. Remember my hole-in-the-shoe story? Ask about the hole first. How did it get there? How long has it been there? When did you notice the hole? *Don't try to fix it yet*! You want to establish the current condition of the business first. Two things will happen after the condition questions are completed:

1) You have a potential prospect who might be up to changing and buying.
2) You do not have a prospect.

You see, sometimes you meet with a decision maker and quickly realize you can't help her, or what she already has in place is something you can't improve upon. Once you spend an appropriate amount of time finding out how they do or use things currently, you'll be able to tell if you need to continue on in the sales process or end the meeting with class and dignity. Most often, you will find areas where what you are bringing to the table can improve their current situation. The next step is to ask some challenge questions to uncover and help them see the problems that may be occurring.

Challenge Questions

These questions are designed to uncover possible problems with the current conditions of the company. Challenge questions are at their best when they are asked open-ended.

Samples

- What steps do you have to take when your present system fails?
- How do you handle the customers when the waiting time becomes longer than normal?
- How often do you have to discard products not up to standard?
- Why does the bank take forty-eight hours to process your funds?
- When the vendor is late or doesn't show, what are the steps you take?

- How do you handle customers that can't pay by your method of payments?
- When cash flow is tight, how do you handle payroll?
- Why is 27 percent of your receivables past 120 days?

After a study of how the company operates now, these *challenge questions* come from areas of possible "problems" you have identified in that exploration. Challenge questions build on the current procedure in place at the company. They uncover indefinite needs that the decision maker may not be aware of, or needs that may not have risen to the level of concern. When you are asking these questions, it allows the decision maker to actually verbalize the problems out loud. When it comes out of the decision maker's mouth, it carries more weight and value versus *you* telling *them* what the problems might be.

That is the power of asking good questions! Don't forget, people buy when they see the need *and* want to do something about it. Your next line of questions is designed to move her from not only seeing the need but also to use you sooner rather than later to make it better. Now it's time for the consequence questions.

Consequence Questions

These questions are designed to move the prospect from indefinite need to definite need and create a sense of urgency to improve the current conditions of the company. Consequence questions are at their best when they are asked open-ended.

Samples

- What impact does it have on your customers when the system is down constantly?
- When payroll is always in a flux, how does it affect the morale of your employees?
- What impact does it have on your sales when forms of payment are limited?

- What is the effect on your profitability when you have to constantly pay overtime?
- How does it affect your business having a 40 percent turnover rate?
- What are the risks of not having a formal risk management process in place?
- What are the consequences when expense control is not managed accurately?
- Why do you feel you're struggling with connecting with your target audience?
- How does that affect your customers?
- If this problem persists, what do you do?

The ramifications or impact of areas you've identified as possible concerns is where you begin to move that prospect to definite need. This is where she starts to agree that a change might be best. You've explored (conditions questions) what the company is currently doing. You've then identified a few areas (challenges questions) where you think you might bring some value and asked if there might be possible problems.

Now you've asked about the ramifications (consequences questions) of these areas causing some concern. Is it now time to jump into your sales pitch of all the glorious solutions you have? Not yet! The power is *still* in the asking of the questions. Don't forget, when it comes from their mouth, it is fact. When it comes from your mouth, it is still under speculation. Move to the final step, *change questions*!

Change Questions

These questions are designed to get the prospect to move forward with specific next steps and acquiring your products or services. Change questions are at their best when they are asked open-ended.

Samples

- Would increasing your revenue stream by 20% be something you would like to do?

- If you could decrease the expense with your present method, why would you not do so?
- Is this way better than what you're currently doing?
- If you could cut the time to move those products, would that improve productivity?
- What would you do with that extra income?
- Which of your employees would benefit from this the most?
- Do you think changing this process would increase your profit margins?
- Would you like to hear how we can make it better?

If you have followed the steps I have described above and have really taken the time to understand each type of question and why you are asking it and what you want to get from it, then you are on your way to even better success. In theory, once you have gotten the information of how the business does things now, what possible problems may be occurring within that process, the ramifications and consequences from those problems continuing to exist, and verbal responses from the prospect on how it could and should be better, then you are on your way to securing more business!

By the way, this is not easy to master in a short time. It will take you a while to first learn the types of questions specific to your product or service. Then you must learn to weave them in their proper order. Then you must do it a few dozen times in presentation to get comfortable with it. Guess what? You already are pretty good at two of the four types of sales questions already: condition and change.

See, most salespeople fall into the mistake of giving information before getting information. Translation: they talk too much. Let's go visit the sales psychiatrist again! Many salespeople are so excited that they actually secured the meeting. Finally, someone who wants to listen to my spiel! And after a quick introduction, they ask a few quick questions (of which the majority are close-ended), and then they are off to the races waxing poetic about themselves, their company, and their products and services. End result: not great.

Here is the path *many* salespeople take:

- Condition questions > Change questions
- Result = Low success rate

Here is the path *great* salespeople take:

- Condition questions > Challenge questions > Consequence questions > Change questions
- Result = High success rate

Many salespeople forget the two types of questions that move the prospect from indefinite need to definite need. The challenge questions and the consequence questions are *critical.* They are also the ones that are harder to ask and take the most time learning to use effectively. We are all good at the first and last types of questions. We do it all the time. But those *middle two* are where you make the difference between a few sales a month or more sales a month.

- Are you a sales representative?
- How often do you have months where you don't reach or exceed your goals?
- How does it impact you financially or professionally when you fail to meet those goals?
- If using the four-step questioning process could help you achieve your goals more often, would you try it?

See? I Just Used the Process on You!

A fatal flaw of many salespeople is they underestimate the power of asking questions. The more questions you ask, the longer you stay in control. The more you are able to really listen and look for things that can help you justify the purchase of your product or service and the more the words are coming out of your prospect's mouth than yours, the better your chances of getting what you need out of the meeting.

When you learn the four steps of finding out what is going on in their businesses, the possible problems that may exist, the ramifications of those problems, and the positive change you can bring, then you are going to become even more successful than you are right now. At the beginning of this chapter, I mentioned *The Practice.* The skill the lawyers displayed by asking the "right" questions to try to bring that "prospect" to the desired end kept my attention. Now it's your time *to practice* this questioning pathway. It will take some time to master it, but you can do it!

Chapter 7

The Reason Not to Give Up

I love movies. There is nothing better than going to the movie theater, armed with a big bag of overpriced popcorn and equally overpriced Coca-Cola, and becoming immersed in a good film. I tend to have a diverse palate when it comes to the types of movies I enjoy. I can relish a superhero flick, especially those that feature Captain America. I appreciate a solid drama. I delight in a good comedy movie, especially when it is clever. I don't like comedies that are easy and go for the cheap jokes.

Nothing beats a good scary movie—not the slasher types that are tawdry, but the ones that just keep you and leave you in a state of unease. Sign me up for any film based on war and true events in that category. I do have a few genres that are not my taste: movies that take place in a submarine or a plane, films where everyone is always in the same clothes and seem to never take a shower, flicks about racing cars all over the world, and not too interested in political-intrigue movies.

Probably my favorite genre, and it's like having to choose a favorite child, is biographical movies. I love movies that explore the lives of historical people. It is interesting to me to learn about their backgrounds, the challenges or hardships they faced, and all the events that led up to who they eventually became and how I know of them today. Some movies of note, in my opinion, are *Chaplin, Schindler's List, Lincoln, Under the Sea* (Bobby Darin biopic,) and *We Were Soldiers.* There are dozens more. Every now and then, a good made for TV movie rears its head.

It fits perfect with where I want to go within this chapter. It's a 2002 made-for-TV movie entitled *Door to Door*. There is a good chance that you have never heard of it. The movie stars William H. Macy, Kyra Sedgwick, Helen Mirren, Michael Shanks, and Kathy Baker. The film is about a real-life person named Bill Porter, played by William H. Macy.

Bill Porter, who sadly passed away in 2013, was an American salesman for the real-life company, Watkins Incorporated. Watkins is based out of Winona, Minnesota. Joseph Ray Watkins started the company by selling liniments door-to-door. Watkins went on to become a very successful company and broadened their scope of product lines from health-care remedies to baking goods and more. Two additional interesting notes is: 1) it is believed that the Watkins Company was the first company in America to offer the "money-back guarantee"; 2) in 2018, Watkins entered into the Guinness Book of World Records for "greatest number of layers in a cake." I know you're wondering, so it consisted of 260 layers!

Bill Porter was an amazing man. He was born in San Francisco, California, in September of 1932. He was the only child of a housewife and sales clerk. He was also born with cerebral palsy. At a young age, his mother and he moved to Portland, Oregon. He has said that he wasn't allowed to brood over his disability. His right side of his body was twisted and his speech was garbled. His mother was the ultimate optimist. She insisted that Bill be the same way.

His first introduction to public school came when he reached seventeen and was enrolled by his mom in high school. After he graduated, his father insisted that he get a job. As you might imagine, this was probably easier said than done. For over four months, he tried *daily* to get a job. He was rejected every day for over sixteen weeks. He had used the help of an employment agency, and after all this time, they advised him to just go home and collect welfare.

He decided to ignore that and began searching through the want ads in the local newspaper. Ultimately, he applied for a job at Watkins Incorporated, the country's oldest door-to-door sales company. He had to convince Watkins that he could do the job. Watkins, to their credit, offered him a job. However, they assigned him to the worst territory and offered to pay him commission only. Each day, Bill Porter would wake up at 4:45 a.m. before catching a 7:30

a.m. bus. You see, he needed ninety minutes to dress himself. Among other things, he could not button his shirts or attach his clip-on tie.

He would then connect to a second bus to have him in his territory by 9:00 a.m. He would return routinely after 7:00 p.m. each night. He packed a lunch bag, and his mother would always leave a note of positivity in it. To say that he was rejected a lot would be an understatement. He had doors slammed in his face, or people that even refused to open the door. When this happened, he would repeat to himself, "The next customer will say yes."

By all accounts, he was relentless and never took the rejection personally. He swore never to give up and "worked" on some of his customers to buy his products for *years.* Want to know how committed Bill Porter was? One time, during an ice storm, he crawled the last part of his route on his hands and knees. He was asked how, or better why, did you do this? He said it was one of his best days he ever had selling. More people were home thanks to the storm.

Bill Porter went on to work for Watkins Incorporated for fifty years. He won countless awards and even became a motivational speaker. Once, a reporter for *People Magazine* asked him if he was surprised by all his success and achievements. And after a brief baffled look, he said, "It never entered my mind that I couldn't." Wow. What a story. What lessons. Why was this only a TV movie and not a studio blockbuster?

In the profession of sales, we face a lot of rejection. I have friends and family that used to think I had the coolest job. I traveled all over the country, performing my one-day workshops to adoring crowds. I got to fly in airplanes and stay in hotels. All expenses paid! Sounds like a pretty good deal, right? What those people didn't see is all the work it took to actually find and get ahold of that potential client, work through series of meetings, overcome all the obstacles, agree to the price before I stepped on the airplane, and stay at that hotel to deliver my service. The unseen work of a sales person.

One of the hardest tenants of the sales process is giving up prematurely. This moment of giving up happens in various parts of the process. It could be giving up early in doing good preparation for a call or meeting, giving up prematurely when trying to reach someone over the phone, giving up too quickly on a prospect that seems complacent, and giving up on trying to reach your goal at the end of the month or quarter; worst case, giving up on your career in sales.

I happen to think it's one of the best career choices out there. I remember someone once telling me, "Nothing happens until someone sells something." I could write another whole book on this topic alone. I want to focus now on a very specific area within the sales process that is always at the top of the list of "things salespeople struggle with": overcoming objections and giving up prematurely.

Objections typically happen in two areas of the process:

1) Scheduling the appointment with the prospect or client
2) During the initial and subsequent appointments with the prospect or client

Objections typically come in two types:

1) Invalid objections; these normally happen while *setting* appointments
2) Valid objections: these normally happen *during* appointments

Before we dive into the details of overcoming objections, let's first understand the situations where objections are born and thrive. The earliest situation is when salespeople are trying to schedule the meeting. I need to ask a question. When you contact someone, out of the blue, with no previous interaction or introduction, is it more likely for them to give you immediate resistance over the phone or immediate acceptance?

If you said acceptance, are the people you're calling saying something like, "Well, hello! Where have you been? We've been waiting by the phone for your call. You don't need to say anything further, when am I meeting with you?" Well, if that is the response you get all the time, skip to chapter 8!

If you answer that the vast majority of the time you encounter resistance, then keep reading! Congratulations, you're in the same boat as most sales representatives. Resistance is by far what most people get. You are an unknown person, calling for an unknown product and service. You're shocked that you get immediate resistance? Learn to expect the resistance!

This shouldn't come as a surprise to you one bit. When you dial the number to a business prospect and adroitly navigate the gatekeeper, and the owner comes to the phone, you should be expecting him to say something like, "I'm not interested." You should also be pleasantly surprised, if he doesn't. Also, the type of objections you get in this situation is invalid objections. They're called invalid objections for a reason.

The next situation is objections that occur during the actual meetings. After mastering your four-step questioning process, they may become fewer and farther between, but they will still ensue. These valid objections come during the actual conversation when the decision maker is engaged in the dialogue. In the earlier part of the meeting, he may be wavering between indefinite need and definite need, so the objection is likely due to him rationalizing between what he has now versus what you are presenting as another option. More often, the objections come nearer the end of the meeting when it comes to things like pricing, structuring, and implementation. Typically, the objections are more valid.

Here's an example. Invalid objection: "I'm not interested." Valid objection: "That price is too high." The invalid objection has *no* weight behind it *or* before it happens. The valid objection has *more* weight behind it because there has been *more* discovery dialogue before it happens. Overcoming both types of objections is critical to improving your results in sales. So know the situation, know the type of objection you are overcoming, and know that they're going to come at you, whether you want them to or not.

I now want to lay out the process of how, when, and why objections occur. I will first describe handling the invalid objections. Invalid objections can happen any time, but most often occur while trying to schedule the appointment. Objections happen both with business prospects and clients. For the purpose of illustration, I will use the scenario of calling a business.

When calling a potential business prospect, you can expect invalid objections first from the gatekeeper and then once you get ahold of the decision maker. Regardless of which scenario it is, the process is the same. The first element is the fact that when the call is received, the process starts by the *interruption*. When that call is answered by either the gatekeeper or the decision maker, the first thing to understand is you are interrupting them. This call is unexpected. If you have ever felt that you are "bothering them," you are.

After the interruption happens and you introduce yourself and your company, the second factor appears: *resistance*. This is where the called individual realizes that this is an "unknown" entity, no familiarity, and their resistance starts to rise. I attest that you can hear it in their voice when they say something like, "Yes. What is it that you need?" When you then tell them that you would like to speak to the decision maker (if it's the gatekeeper) or ask for the appointment (if it's the decision maker), the next thing that happens is they give you what I call a *reflex no*.

Why do I call it a reflex no? Because it pops out instantly and usually carries very little or no weight. The word "reflex" means a spontaneous effect, an impulse. It's also most likely an invalid objection. As you well know, businesses get inundated with sales calls. And what are they almost conditioned to say automatically? "We're good." "I'm not interested." "She's busy right now." "Send me some information." "I don't need anything right now." Guess what? These are all invalid objections; another phrase you might have heard before, "blow-offs."

What do you think many sales representatives do at this moment? They give up! They say something like, "Well, sorry to have bothered you. Maybe I'll call back in a few months and see how you're doing." What? Would Bill Porter have done that? I highly doubt it. Bill would have realized that this was a conditioned reflexive response and would have continued trying to secure the meeting.

Let's be brutally honest: If you're going to give up the first time someone throws out an invalid objection that they impulsively say every time they hear from a sales person, why call them in the first place? I think it's the same outcome. Instead, you need to follow the last two tenets of the objection process. You have to be able to *respond* to the objection. You do not have to give a response worthy of Shakespeare, but a good, concise, and logical response that fits their objection. Use your common sense. Come up with a go-to response for the most common objections you get, and memorize it and use it!

> *Example*
>
> Decision Maker: I'm too busy for appointments.
>
> Your Response: I can appreciate that you are working with a tight schedule. Maybe we could meet before 8:00 a.m. or after 6:00 p.m.?

So far so good; you're almost there! Sadly, this is where many sales representatives stop! They give some sort of response and then wait for the other person to decide what to do. What did we learn earlier? The person *asking the questions* is in control. You're not done handling the objection until you add the final part. You must now *request action.*

The request for action is always in the form of a question. This forces the other to answer and keeps you in charge. Let me use a tennis analogy. Imagine that you are playing a game of tennis, and the decision maker is on one side of the net and you on the other. She "hits" that objection over the net to you. In tennis, you have to do two things to be successful. First, you must *respond* to where the ball is going to be landing in your court. Once you get there, you can't just stare at it and watch it go by; you will lose the point! You have to get your racket on the ball and "request action" back onto her side of the court! Of course, you need to be ready in case she hits another one at you.

Example

DECISION MAKER: I'm too busy for appointments.

YOUR RESPONSE: I can appreciate that you are working with a tight schedule. Maybe we could meet before 8:00 a.m. or after 6:00 p.m.?

YOUR REQUEST ACTION: Could we get together, say, Tuesday morning at 7:30 a.m.?

The flow chart of the objection process looks like this:

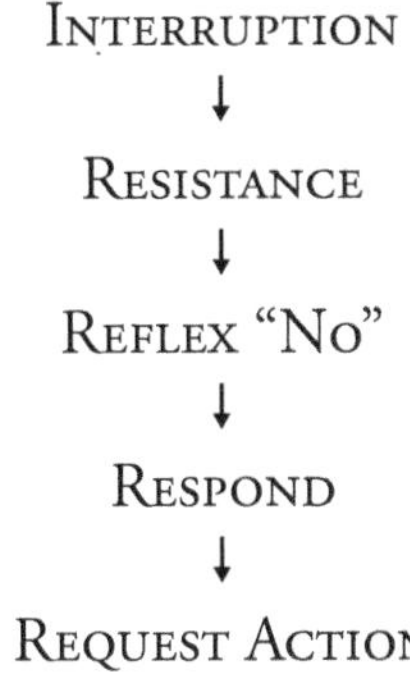

This same process is followed when you call an existing client. You call and *interrupt* them; their *resistance* goes up after they see that it is you and not their buddy. You ask to meet, and they give you some sort of *reflex* "no." Then you need to both *respond* and *request action.*

Did you know that you probably experience this flow chart in your ordinary life without realizing you're in it? Let me share an experience I had recently and refer back to the above chart as you digest the story.

Not too long ago, my wife and I went to the mall. She was going to be in a wedding in a few months and needed to get the required bridesmaid attire. While she was doing that, I figured I would look around for a new tie as I was attending the wedding with her. So I parted ways and headed to Dillards. If you're not familiar with Dillards, it's an American department store chain with approximately 282 stores in twenty-nine states and headquartered in Little Rock, Arkansas. I love Dillards.

I walked over to the men's section and began looking through their tables of ties. After a few minutes, I happened to look up and saw a Dillard's employee just finishing up with a customer and, after he did, made eye contact with me. At that brief moment, we were both kind of just looking at each other: *interruption*.

He saw that I was by myself and started to head over to where I was. As he approached, my *resistance* naturally began rising. I thought to myself, *Oh no, he's coming to me.* When he finally arrived, he said, "Can I help you with something?" Now what do we *all* say at this moment when it happens to us, all the time, without any hesitation? We give a classic *reflex* "no." I said, "Oh, I'm just kind of browsing."

Sadly, he did what many salespeople do. He gave up too quickly. In fact, right off the bat. He said, "Well, my name is Avery, and if you need me, I'll be over here in the shoe section." He left. I looked around and didn't see anything that caught my eye, and I walked right out of Dillards and back into the mall. He didn't sell anything; I didn't buy anything. Lose-lose. Does this mean this sales rep was terrible and Dillards is never to be shopped again? Of course not! He did what we *all* do on a regular basis.

So I headed down past the food court, made a left, and went into Macys. The same exact scenario played out. I was looking through Macys' table of ties. The Macys rep came over to me and asked me the same exact question the Dillards person did. "Can I help you with something?" I gave him the same answer I gave the Dillards' associate. "Oh, I'm just browsing." Guess what?

The Macys sales associate played a little figurative tennis. He was ready to *respond* and said, "Well, I noticed you're looking at some of our ties. We have a brand-new shipment that just came in. In fact, I haven't even opened the box yet." He then put that racket on the ball and hit it right to me with a *request* for *action*. He added, "Would you like to take a look at some of the new ones that just came in?"

I responded by saying, "Sure, I'll take a look at them." It didn't mean I was going to buy anything, but he was able to move the process forward, and literally me, to the counter. He could have spread all the ties out on the counter, and I may not have found one that interested me, and I could have left the store. The same result if he had just given up the minute I said, "I'm just browsing."

However, he presented the new ties on the counter and, lo and behold, right there in the middle, was a midnight-blue tie. First of all, my favorite color. Second of all, that color is very difficult to find. Last of all, I thought it would look great with my grey suit and a crisp-white shirt. Guess what's hanging in my closet? Was he pushy? No. Was he great at playing a little sales tennis? Yes.

When you finally have the *appointment* with the client or decision maker, you are more likely to run into more *valid* objections. These objections carry a little more "weight" to them. In years of selling and training, I have learned that there are four times that you can handle objections: 1) when they come up; 2) before they come up; 3) after they come up; and 4) never. So let's look at the most common time these valid objections occur, and that is *when* they happen.

Someone asks you early on a question or gives some sort of early objection about your product or service, you're going to answer that right then and there and continue on. The second time you may handle an objection is *before* it comes up. What comes up in *any* sales situation, whether you're selling a service or product? "How much does it cost?" So knowing this, you want to be able to bring it up *before* they bring it up. For example, toward the end of your presentation, you might say something like, "Based upon what we've talked about here, the best part about all this, it's only $_______." So now you've done it before they come with the question about price. You are probably familiar with the "common" objections you get from your targeted audience, so learn how to address it before it becomes an objection! Incidentally, these also may be just questions that tend to come up. Answer the questions if you have to or answer them before they ask! If they come in the form of questions, that a good sign because it seems to show some level of interest.

So now you've addressed it before they come up with an objection about price. Another time to answer these questions and objections is *after* they come up. During your presentation, the prospect may be asking you a number of questions about your product or service. Rather than continuing to answer these questions or handling any objections throughout, you know in your presentation that you're going to address that specific concern. So you could simply say, "You know, that's a great question, and as we go through this, I think you will see how we address that very detail."

The last way to handle these objections is never. I don't mean this to be something done in a condescending way. More in the sense that sometimes people make statements to you. And when they make statements to you, they are just that, and they don't really need your attention. "Oh, that's a lot of money." Move on. "Oh, you're just a sales person." Move on. "The last guy in here offered me this and that." That is fantastic. So do you want this?

You know your business better than me. You know the targeted prospects you want to try to work. You've made several presentations in your career. You almost certainly have heard similar objections in many of those meetings. If you know the usual objections you get, why not try to address them *before* they happen? If you have to answer them *when* or *after* they come up, do so.

I will tell you, when you start to master the four-step questioning process we covered in the previous chapter, you can eliminate many of them there. As an example, when you're in the area of costs and pricing in the meeting, you might ask a good challenge question like, "What are the risks associated with always choosing a service because of a lower rate or price?" Let *them* tell you the risks of doing so. Then they have vocalized those risks, and when you get to your price quote, it's a bit harder to argue because you already have their talking points on what the risks are and maybe some benefits of paying a little more to get an added product or service.

I really revel and have used often the *never* option. Truthfully, it's the rarest, but effective in its use. As an illustration, when I was selling for TeleCheck, we were trained to get a 150-dollar set-up fee at the time of signing the merchant up for our services. The good news was we got to keep half of the fee as commission. With the expectation of bringing on fifteen new merchants a month, that was

$1,125 possible extra commission we could receive! That's $13,500 annually. All we had to do was simply say something like, "So all I need to do now is get the 150-dollar installment fee, and we can begin the process of making you our next new client."

First of all, what is sad is *many* of our sales reps would wave or greatly discount that fee. They would give away that commission just to get the deal. Of course, the bulk of the commissions for them were in the deal. But to leave $13,500 on the table? Where is that sales psychiatrist again? I think the main reason was they couldn't comfortably answer the "objection" that they thought they got from the merchant. "One hundred fifty-dollar set-up fee sure seems high." Okay, let me just waive it for you. Ouch!

To begin with, this isn't an objection. This is a statement. That fee seems high. You can still use the never technique here. "Would you like to pay it by check now, or would billing it on your first invoice be more convenient?" If the merchant was saying an actual objection, it would be more like, "The 150-dollar set-up fee is too high." Never time! "You can pay it now by check, or we will conveniently add it to your first invoice." I would watch them pause, and many times say, "Put it on the invoice." The more "matter-of-fact" you are, the more normal it feels, and the less resistant they are.

So there are some quick ideas around the "when, before, after, and the never," but, as I said, most often, you will deal with the "when" when the objection happens. Ironically, you will follow the flow chart of handling objections with just a few modifications. When you have a scheduled meeting, obviously you are not interrupting them. They have agreed to the meeting. This helps because that also means their resistance should be mitigated a bit, or they most likely would not have agreed to the meeting in the first place.

Subsequently, you (hopefully) begin your presentation following the questioning process to start to move them from indefinite need to definite need. The prospect or client should be engaged in the dialogue with you now. And through this exploration, he or she has more time to think through process and scenario and implications and ramifications, which may formulate a more valid objection.

The reflex “no,” which is highly instantaneous, is replaced with a more calculated “no.”

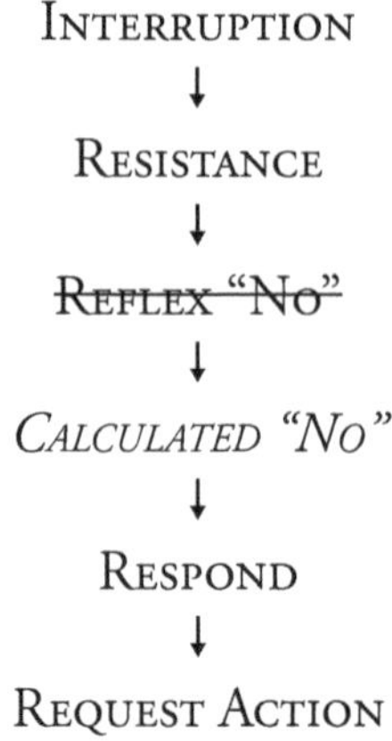

Example

Decision Maker: The price is just too high.

Your Response: When you say the price is too high, what are you comparing it to? (Wait for the answer.) Oftentimes, the price doesn’t relate to the overall cost. Remember when you said there seemed to be some other fees with your current provider?

Request Action: Could we take a few minutes and compare the cost?

The *key* to overcoming more *invalid* objections is to respond and then request action.

The *key* to overcoming more *valid* objections is to be sharp in your need’s assessment using the four-step questioning process and also be able to respond and then request action. *When a prospect gets to definite need, she has less objections. When she is still stuck in indefinite need, she has more objections.*

Finally, as it relates to overcoming objections, the question begs: "How many should I handle, before I give up?" The answer is very simple when you are calling just to secure the appointment: three! Not one, not eleven. Three. Don't forget, these are reflexive objections. When you get the first one, respond and request action. Do the same with the second and third. If the client or prospect gives you a fourth objection, that is your cue to politely and professionally end the call. "Thanks, Ms. Hughes, for giving me some time to speak with you. I will follow up with you periodically to make sure we are meeting your needs. Have a great rest of the week." Then pick up the phone and call the next client! The means to the end here is to hang in there for three objections *if* the objections are *diminishing* in their intensity.

Here's an example:

FIRST CLIENT OBJECTION: I'm not interested.
YOU: Respond > Request action

SECOND CLIENT OBJECTION: Well, send me some information to my email, and I'll look it over.
YOU: Respond > Request action

THIRD CLIENT OBJECTION: I really should speak with my spouse first.
YOU: Respond > Request action

See how the objections are softening? That's your cue to hang in there. Don't stop until you handle three. You're getting closer to scheduling the appointment! Now, are there exceptions to the rule of three? Yes. *If* the client's objections start to stay constant in their intensity or, worse, starting to escalate in their intensity, then you're allowed to let him go! And then, of course, call the next prospect or client on your list!

Here's an example:

Prospect Objection: I'm not interested.
You: Respond > Request action

Prospect Objection: Did you hear what
I said? I am not interested!
You: Not a problem, sir, thanks for taking a
minute with me. Have a great day.

You don't have to beg anyone to work with you or buy your products and services. The value you bring to your clients and the value your company brings its clients is sufficient for whomever you call. As you know, some people will set a meeting with you. A much larger group will not. Welcome to sales.

As far as the number of objections one should take in the actual meeting, my initial reaction is to trust your gut. The goal here is to limit the number of objections that might arise in the first place. As already mentioned, the better skill you employ engaging that prospect into a real dialogue, where they are doing most of the talking and you are asking the questions and doing the most listening, is best.

If you do your work finding out what is going on in their business now, any problems or challenges that might be present due to those conditions in place, the consequences and ramifications of such problems continuing to exist, then when you get to the closing and making the change questions, your liability to objections should be greatly reduced. Not eliminated, reduced.

I've worked hard to position the meeting where I've covered all the challenges that I know might exist from my experiences in working with similar companies. When done correctly, the objections I have faced are few. I can't underscore enough; this reality happens when the prospect is readily engaged in the conversation. If not, more objections are sure to come.

Two last bonus pieces of advice. First, learn the difference between a question and an objection. They are handled differently.

An objection requires a response and a request for action. A question just needs an answer without having to defend it. The second piece of advice is if you are getting multiple objections during your presentation, it is most likely the result of failing in the initial step of needs analysis and not asking a sufficient amount of *condition questions.*

Here is a classic example:

PROSPECT OBJECTION: I don't do sales calls (i.e., not interested).
YOU: Respond > Request action

PROSPECT QUESTION: Is this a sales call?
YOU: Yes, sir, it is!

Bill Porter exemplifies the reason not to give up. He had doors slammed in his face or people that even refused to open the door. When this happened, he would repeat to himself, "The next customer will say yes." He took objection after objection in person, over the phone, and to prospects and clients alike. I think he even handled a lot more objections than just three.

The reason you don't give up in any part of the sales process boils down to two things: First, you believe in yourself and your company enough to know that you, and it, will honestly work and sell to people the things that can truly make their lives or companies better than before you walked in their door or called them on the phone. And two, you know that the customer or prospect doesn't realize this until they are able to understand how this can be a reality. So for *their* sake, don't give up on them.

Chapter 8

The Lost Art of Trial Closes

John Gehegan is the owner and founder of Gehegan & Associates. John was born in Bronx, New York. As a kid growing up in the Bronx, he learned how to hustle. As a natural leader at a very young age, he learned how to get a stickball game going with his friends after school and on weekends. Shortly after completing his undergraduate degree at Iona College in New Rochelle, New York, he moved to beautiful California and started a career in sales with Lanier Office Products.

A natural sales person, he moved up quickly within the company. As a manager, he led his team to new heights and taught them everything he knew about being successful in their sales habits. He designed trainings and seminars to keep his team sharp and working like a well-oiled machine. Seeing his own strengths and love of being able to train and coach salespeople, he decided to leave Lanier and start his own sales training firm.

One of the members of his sales team left and started working for a bank in southern California. Not too long after, he called his former favorite boss and asked him if he could put something together for his current group of bankers. John was delighted to help. Soon, with word of mouth and heavy prospecting all by himself, I might add, Gehegan & Associates began to take off and is now one of the most respected training firms within the financial institution business.

John's relentless effort has allowed him to train sales associates from the Philippines to the United Arab Emirates and everywhere in between. He has personally trained just over one hundred thousand salespeople from all walks of life and all types of sales organizations. He is quite an amazing sales person. He is the best trainer I have ever witnessed, and I've seen hundreds.

I think what separates John Gehegan from most others is he is not only the teacher, but he is also an avid student of the sales process. He ruminates on the process endlessly. He constantly looks for new and different ways to enhance, not only his skills but also the skills of others. Armed with a deep intelligence of the sales process and a razor-sharp sense of humor, he handles any group with ease. Most importantly, they walk out of any training he does with new energy, confidence, and the willingness to go back to their respective offices and change the way they have been doing things to be more successful.

John and I got to know each other back in 1992. I was a brand-new sales representative, and I, like all the others, learned my entire sales process from him. He was the sales vendor for our company, TeleCheck. I can tell you that it worked out great for me. In fact, it worked out great for most all of our salespeople. When First Data Corporation acquired TeleCheck around 1995, the TeleCheck salespeople became some of the top sales representatives for the entire company. That is still true today.

After a successful stint in sales, I was quickly promoted to area manager. I then went on to become one of the corporate sale trainers for the company. I ended my career as district manager for one of the top districts in all of TeleCheck. It was during my time as the corporate training manager at the TeleCheck headquarters that I really got to know John. We had sales reps all over the US, Canada, and Australia. Part of my duties was to bring in these reps to go through what we called Gehegan I and Gehegan II. These were the two classes where our reps learned the methods to become great salespeople.

I sat in the back of the room for dozens of classes, watching John work with the teams. He went through the entire sales process from the moment they called or walked into a business until the deal was closed. You would think after viewing several classes I would have just "checked out" or left to do other things while he instructed the classes. Honestly, every time I observed, I picked up something new. I was taking notes just like them.

One day after a class, I went up to John and told him that I wanted to do what he was doing. In that, I meant that I might try to start my own business like what he had done. He said that he would be glad to talk with me, and we set dinner plans for the following evening. During that dinner, he said that he thought about my interest in doing what he was doing. Then, as only he could do, he started using his sales skills on me.

He asked about all that I was *currently doing*, the *challenges* that came with it, how it was *impacting* me now as far as what I wanted to accomplish in my career, and how would this *change* be beneficial in bringing that about. He was doing the four-step questioning with me in the middle of a restaurant! He also was tossing in a few other questions that I have realized have become a lost art: trial-close questions. At the end of my "sales meeting," he asked if I would just like to work with him. I've been working with him now for over twenty years. I guess you know what my answer was.

It has been said that if you ever want to get some real rest, don't do it in a hospital. Why is that so true? I don't know if you have ever been in the hospital overnight, or for a few days, but you don't really get to sleep much. The nurses come in every few hours, checking your vitals. How is the patient's temperature? Is the blood pressure okay? How's the oxygen level? Is it time to change the IV bag? How's the wound healing? What do you want for breakfast, lunch, and dinner?

Just when you're about to finally doze off, they are back again, checking to make sure the patient is moving in the right direction! As an analogy to the sales process, we should be checking the "temperature" of the prospect or client along the way during our sales presentations. Sadly, many don't. It is a simple and effective tool that can increase the buy-in from your potential buyer.

John does this effectively. If truth be told, to this day, when we are on calls, he reminds me to do it. We will be on a conference call with a client, and my cell phone text notifications will illuminate. Ask them this! What about this? I have learned to do the same with him. Not that he needs any reminder.

Here is an actual screenshot of what he did during one of our recent conference calls, not all the questions are trial-close questions, but you see a few sprinkled in:

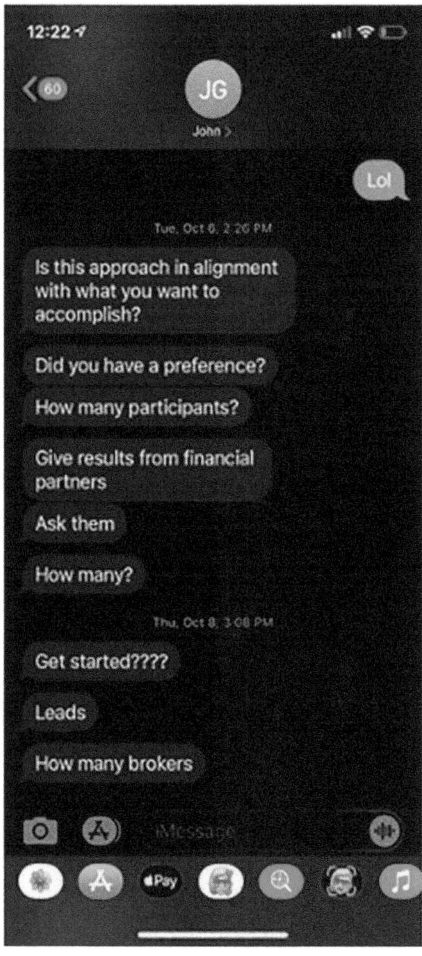

Consider what I have covered before. The buyer buys when she sees a definite need and wants to do something about it. And what comes out of the buyer's mouth, to her, is fact. They instinctively believe. What comes from the seller's mouth can always be challenged or disbelieved because the buyer may not be able to determine a need exists, or may believe that it *might* exist, but isn't that big of a deal.

Trial-close questions can gauge the level of the buyer's interest or level of agreement of the problem that your solution(s) can eliminate or mitigate. So sprinkled in your presentation should be some of the questions to check the "pulse" of your "patient." A trial-close question is different from the change or "close" question. Think of the change questions as more final, ending, or concluding. The trial-close questions are more of an examination, experiment, or tryout. They are more like the audition, rather than securing the part.

Trial-close questions are often thought of as questions as you are nearing the end of the meeting or conversation; the close before the close, if you will. However, they are more effective if they are used *throughout* the conversation! Remember the nurses? They check *throughout* the night and day. They can't just wait until the day the patient is going to be discharged to "see how they did." They have to know along the way so they can make changes to get the best result.

In your sales presentations, the trial closes can be used to gauge how the buyer is coming through the process. Is he seeing what you're seeing? Is he thinking through it with you and applying what you're discussing in a meaningful way to be open to changing things and hiring you?

Sample Trial Close Questions

- Is this better than what you're doing now?
- Would this make the process run smoother?
- Would your customers benefit more if you did it this way?
- Is this easier?
- What would your employees think about this change?
- What are the benefits of doing it this way?
- Will this increase your cashflow?
- How does this sound so far?
- Is this in alignment of what you want to accomplish?
- Is this something you should do sooner rather than later?
- How would doing it this way be more convenient?
- Would this be helpful?
- Is this an improvement?

As you weave through your presentation, it is a best practice to look for every opportunity to gain "buy-in" from your client or prospect. One of our associates has even named them "opinion prompts." A lot of salespeople do their presentation, ask for questions at the *end*, and then try to close the sale. The only one buying in this format is the one who already has figured out that there is a definite need. Probably a good chance, they called you!

To be more successful, conduct a presentation where the foremost goal is to engage in a reciprocal dialogue. As you control the dialogue with good questions and answers, add some "opinion prompts" along the full path of the conversation. Let's look at a scenario of how trial closes can be effective in moving that potential client to definite need and your next sale:

Scenario

The meeting is with the owner of a two-location restaurant. His servers still take the food orders by hand at the table and walk the ticket to the kitchen.

Condition question asked by seller:
"How do your servers currently take orders from your clientele?"
Buyer's answer:
"They take the orders from the table on their pads and take the orders to the kitchen."
Challenge question asked by seller:
"What happens if the customer changes their order after the kitchen has received it?"
Buyer's answer:
"If it can't be quickly used, we must waste it."
Consequence question asked by seller:
"How is that impacting your bottom line if you have that happening several times a week?"
Buyer's answer:
"It's just a cost of doing business that we account for."

Trial-close question asked by seller:
"What would you invest in your business with that lost revenue by eliminating this from happening?"
Buyer's answer:
"I probably would invest in whatever it is that could help stop this from occurring."
Change question asked by seller:
"Would you like to see how we can go about eliminating this from happening?"
Buyer's answer:
"I'm open to hearing about it."

Obviously, this is just an example of how the trial close is to be used and not indicative of a perfect result. Trial closes are designed to gauge the interest of the client and similar to testing to see if this client is following the path you are trying to lead. If the answers to the questions are positive in their response, then you're getting somewhere. If not, then maybe you need to reexplore their current process and challenges and consequences a little deeper or maybe try a different angle.

More often than not, a client or prospect responding in an encouraging manner is a sign that your chances of getting some sort of business is improving. Think about it this way: If your target buyer has answered in the affirmative to all your trial closes, it would almost be almost impossible, or extremely odd, for him to say "no" to what you are offering as a solution. Do those "temperature checks" periodically throughout your presentation. I assure you, the "patient" wants to feel better.

Chapter 9

The Price Versus Cost Paradox

I grew up in Apopka, Florida. Apopka is about sixteen miles northwest of downtown Orlando, Florida. Its name is derived from the Seminole Indian word *ahapopka*, which translates to "potato-eating place." Apopka is referred to as "The Indoor Foliage Capital of the World" due to the vast number of greenhouses and nurseries. It also has the distinction of having had one of the longest full-time mayors in America, John Land. He served for 61.25 years through 2014.

Growing up, my dad was the pastor of the largest church in Apopka. He served for over thirty-seven years. Needless to say, that made me kind of a popular kid in school. You see, because the church was large, we were able to host all the larger events for Apopka High School, like the senior's baccalaureate. So I got to know the mayor, and the principals, and lots of other "important" people around town. When I got to Apopka High School as a student, my principal was Larry Payne. Luckily, we already knew each other before I got there; and because of who I was related to, I steered clear of ending up in his office, except for *good* reasons.

I graduated in 1985 and headed on to Stetson University and finished my degree in speech and theater in 1989. After graduation, I had no real idea of what I was going to do with my "work" life. I caught wind that Mr. Payne had left Apopka High School the year after I graduated and was now charged with starting a brand-new high school in Orlando, near the University of Central Florida. In fact, it was to be named University High School.

So I found his contact information and gave him a call. If he needed a speech or drama teacher, I was available! The school wasn't going to open for another nine months and that was actually helpful because I had to go to UCF and get the educational certification courses required by Orange County Public Schools. To Mr. Payne's credit, he took a chance on me, and I was on the inaugural faculty.

Two years later, Orange County had a reduction in force for teachers (RIFT), and luckily, I wasn't let go, but my classes were cut in half. Back in 1992, my salary was $21,000. Now it had been reduced to $8,900. Before taxes! To say that the students were disappointed that it seemed like all the new, fun teachers had been let go or reduced would be an understatement.

One of my students, Bryan Douglas, came up to me after class one day and said his dad might be able to give me a job. I told him that was nice, believing it was more of a kind gesture. That very weekend, his father called, brought me in for an interview, offered me a job, and hired me on the spot. His dad happened to be Gary Douglas, the southeastern regional president for TeleCheck Services. I had never heard of TeleCheck, and even after the interview, I still didn't have a firm grasp. But he gave me a starting salary of $24,000. That was a whole lot more than $8,900, so I signed up and resolved to figure it all out!

In chapter 3, I gave an overview of TeleCheck and then the later acquisition by First Data. So my sales career began in the world of merchant services. We offered payment processing to merchants across the US and Canada. When I got to my first position as a sales representative, I learned fairly quick that it seemed that all the merchants tended to care or ask about was the rate. What is the rate? I had a price book that listed almost every known business type and the rate associated with it.

Early on, when I got that question, I would just turn to my book and quote whatever rate was there. I was quickly discouraged because every single time I quoted the *price*, the merchant would say something like, "That's too high!" "I already have a lower rate." Being brand-new into sales I would stumble through an answer and say something silly like, "Well, that's what it says here in the book."

Chris, Chris, Chris, how lame that is and was! It wasn't until I was taught later that there was more to it than the *price*. There were two other components: *value* and *cost.*

What Are the Values?

You

Sometimes I think when you're in the corporate world, you get so busy with all the policies, regulations, changes, and overall stress of the work, you lose sight of two very important "values" that can make and keep you successful doing it. One is *your* value, and the other is your *company's* value.

First, what value do *you* bring your customers? If I were to interview some of your clients, what would they say about you? These are important questions that I don't believe we think about much, especially when you've been at it a while. Maybe you are accessible, dependable, you keep your word, you put yourself in their shoes, you have integrity, and you are trustworthy. You genuinely listen, you are a problem-solver, you stay current on your education of products and services and market trends, and you invest time learning their market place and developments in their industry. You actually want to build real relationships with them and not just count them as a number on your "board."

I'll bet the main reason they do business with you is because of you and who you are. Why is this important? When you believe that you are the best, most adept, and responsible person they can deal with, you are most likely the one they will deal with. They trust and like you. Let's be honest, they might just be buying you first, and the service or product you have follows in line. I also believe that your focus on the value you bring should also encourage you to hang in there when the prospect starts to waver on buying what you have or meeting with you in the first place.

For example, when you are first calling to get the meeting; if the prospect starts to say anything similar to "I'm not interested," recall *your* value! Recall the dozens of existing clients you have already secured and wouldn't trade you for anything. *This* prospect has no idea what she is getting—yet! So be confident in hanging in there and scrap to stay in it with her, for if she decides to go ahead and meet, she gets to experience you and all the benefits that *you* bring to the table. You can always humbly state the value you bring without sounding like a narcissist!

Once, I was in an appointment with a colleague, who I have known and worked with for a long time. We had an appointment with a large company that you would know. Let's just say they sell office supplies. We had a very good meeting. On the drive back to our office, we did what I think most good sales representatives do, we debriefed on how we thought the meeting went.

After the normal pleasantries and things, we talked through what we might have done better in the presentation. My partner thought for a moment and then said this, "You know what I think is missing from the presentation?" Naturally, I asked for his thoughts. He continued, "You do a really good job navigating the meeting and laying out all the benefits and *value* of what we can and will do for them. I think what's missing is you don't mention, at all, that they get you.

"You don't mention the tens of thousands of people you've trained, have spent literally, almost three solid years in hotel rooms all over the world, as a testament for your demand. You don't give them enough of the value that you, personally, bring to the table." I thought about what he said for a bit, and in my mind, told myself in justification that I don't really enjoy "bragging on myself." It just isn't in my DNA. It feels awkward. After my cogitation, when I relayed it to him, he simply said, "But is it the truth?" He said that it brings a certain extra kind of value that not many others could bring. And the more I thought about it, the more I figured he was right.

Since then, I myself have gotten better at adding that part to the value proposition. It does bring an added bit of confidence in my meetings. I have worked hard for the last twenty-eight-plus years of selling and training. I am good at what I do. And I will do my best for you. There doesn't seem to be much wrong with that!

Company

Not only do you bring a certain value, but also your company brings a ton of value. Now if you don't believe that, I would ask why you are still working there? What value does your company bring to the table? Financial stability? Integrity? Good standing in the market place? Long time in the industry? Quality products and services? Innovative technologies that help their customers do business with convenience and with overall cost savings? It does, right?

These are many of the values that helped you make the decision to work there in the first place. The company employs good people who want to achieve a common goal: striving to be a leader in their marketplace. I think it would be extremely difficult to work so hard to sell something that you didn't truly believe lived up to its billing.

Why is this so important? Again, it always falls back to the point of confidence and determination. If you honestly believe these two truths, that you bring immense value to the customer's relationship *and* the company brings solid value to it as well, then you should be encouraged to reach out to as many possible prospects so that they can benefit from this value and be more resolved to not give up too quickly if the prospect starts to hesitate via objections in *any* part of the sales process.

Think of it like this: If you give up prematurely when the prospect says they are not interested, you are actually doing them a *disservice* by saying something like, "Okay, I'll check back with you in a few months." Remember, back to that confidence from the literal foundation of the value that both you and your company bring to the table and make yourself say, in essence, "I'm not letting you off that easy! I'm confident that if you give us the chance, it will be one of the best business decisions you make all year." And then request that prospect into action to keep the process going!

The Cost

"So what is the price?" The most uttered phrase in the selling world! In some types of selling, it is the word "rate." What the real question should be is, "So what does this cost?" Although found as synonyms in any Thesaurus, they have very different meanings, especially when it comes to selling services. Many buyers get stuck on the price, when they really should be looking at the overall cost. I have been somewhat astounded that some business owners don't get the difference.

First of all, "What is the rate or price?" can be both good and bad. When it's good, it's a buying signal. People don't normally ask the question if there isn't some type of pondering going on in their heads about maybe taking a harder look at what you may be presenting. However, this question normally comes *after* there has been some discussion and needs assessment work put in, and maybe some benefit has appeared.

When this question appears early, or right off the bat, it is probably a bad signal. You can almost feel that the other person, by asking about rate at the very start, is really saying, "I get these calls every day. Let me humor you by asking the price, and then I'll tell you, as politely as I can, to get lost." Been there? Ha. I've lived there! When buyers only consider rate, it's sometimes hard to get them to continue on long enough to discover the actual cost.

I learned quickly that our "pricing" at TeleCheck was almost always higher than all our competitions. Yet, we were the largest of all the other check-guarantee companies and had more merchants than our number one and two competitors *combined.* So the theoretical question was, Why? We charge more for our services, so why are we the largest? An easy answer was "you get what you pay for."

Sure, other competitors had lower pricing but their service was poorer or they would make up their "losses" on rate by charging the merchant other "fees." As far as services provided, TeleCheck was far and above the competition, and that didn't come from me; that came from the thousands who switched over from their existing processor to us. And as far as customer service was concerned, not only were there large groups of customer services reps within the corporate offices in Houston, Texas, but also each TeleCheck office throughout the US and Canada has service rep personnel who could quickly get out in-person to our clients if needed. That kind of echoes back to that company value thing I mentioned earlier.

So why isn't a lower rate a *good* thing? Simply, rate isn't what you need to worry about. Cost is. For example, the merchant would be charged the lower rate of 1.5 percent versus our rate of 1.75 percent for all check and credit card transactions. Let's assume this small business merchant took in $10,000 of credit card/check business per month. The cheaper rate "cost" the merchant $150 instead of $175 from us. That is a 300-dollar savings per year! Good deal, right? Wrong.

The competitor with the lower rate also charged a 15-dollar statement fee. There was also a .10-dollar transaction fee for each transaction. Since the merchant's average ticket was $25, that was forty transactions! At ten cents a transaction, tack on another $40! The merchant was actually getting "charged" $220 per month. So the *effective rate* was actually 2.20 percent. Our rate had all the other costs built in. They would actually save $540 by going with us at the "higher rate."

Have you stayed at a hotel recently? That $125 a night at a nice hotel near Disney World sounds great! Three hundred seventy-five dollars for three nights to wander the Magic Kingdom? Let's go! Um, check your hotel bill. State tax, city tax, resort fee, parking. Hello $535!

The price is one thing; the cost is a very real *other* thing. Learn to sell people what it's going to cost them. *No* surprises. *No* hidden fees. Isn't it a dreaded response from a buyer that "you didn't tell me about that?" Remember, not everyone is going to buy what you have. Some will still not want to pay the price that you are quoting. If you are consistently doing the activity I've talked about earlier, it will certainly give you a big enough audience to have many of them pay the price you are asking for. A smaller audience makes it harder. Some in either audience may start to haggle with you. The sales term for that is negotiation.

Negotiating

I will submit to you that there are three spots in the sales process to negotiate: before the presentation, during the presentation, and after the presentation. I guess there could be a fourth: to never do it. But that probably fits closer to the "before the presentation spot." When I first started in sales, lost, needing to make things happen to earn my best living, I would agree to anything just to get the deal. Waive this, cut this. Just get the business. Forget all that value stuff I just talked about! There was zero negotiating. If my manager would let me get away with it, I did it. I wanted to make a splash.

Then I started seeing how my peers were making a lot more than I was because they were better at sticking to their guns. I finally got some good sales training, particularly around negotiating. Obviously, increasing my activity to have more "at bats" was foundation number 1. As I have pressed, the more prospects you have, the less pressure you put on yourself and them. The fewer prospects you have, the more pressure you put on yourself (negotiating all the time) and them. Eventually though, you will face negotiating. So what are some tips? I don't have the perfect answers, but I'll give you some advice.

You probably know the fundamental rule of negotiation. The best negotiation is when each party feel like they both win. In other words, win-win. Each side feels like the other side has been fair. I have been around and watched others who have the win-lose mentality. "I'm not budging!" "Take it or leave it"—kind of like when you try to feel superior walking off a car lot. If both you and your buyer negotiate together for the greater good, each party walks away feeling like they got what they wanted or needed for a fair outcome. Might this bode well for future engagement with that buyer? Maybe it can open up other pathways in the future. Referrals, anyone? The goal is to win-win.

Let's explore those three times to win-win: before, during, and after. There is good evidence to suggest that the final prices tend to be higher when the seller sets the price versus the buyer offering the price. So the first tip would be to make the offer first. But how do I do that *before* negotiating? You should obviously go into the presentation with a proposal ready of what the quote is going to be.

However, during your preparation for the quote, is this quote going to be negotiable? Some sellers set the price up because they realize they might have to negotiate, so they create wiggle room. So the price you wished they would have bought is negotiated down. Ever walk out of a call and thought to yourself, *They probably would have paid more.*

In your determination of price, predetermine what the reasonable value of what you're providing is. When you have that number, that is your fair-asking price. Some people mark it up by like 25 percent to 35 percent; again, for that wiggle room. Don't misunderstand; charge the price you need to charge. But if your price is already at the "win" spot for your part of the "win-win," then that's when you stand your ground. John Gehegan is the best at this. We spend hours coming up with the price for our future clients and try to make it the fairest price, *in advance*, for what the prospect will be presented. In other words, we already try to make it a "win-win" going into it.

Surely, most organizations do, but do it *consciously.* Do it purposefully. We try to put the best offer forward first. Then we know that there is no room to come down, and it gives the confidence to hold firm. In fact, when the prospect asks us how much it's going to cost, his standard line is, "Well, that's the best part about it. It's only going to be 'X' amount." If you set something higher than you think you're going to get, you're setting yourself up for getting lower than what you thought you might. Whoever starts the offer first is usually the one with the advantage. If you prepare with this mindset, putting the offer together, all the better.

Negotiating *during* the presentation is hard. In fact, true negotiating during a presentation doesn't happen that often. It's hard to negotiate what you haven't finished hearing about and what all else is involved. My feeling on this is, if negotiating starts happening in the middle of the presentation, it could be a good sign; but more likely, it's not a good sign.

You haven't even reached the middle half of the presentation, and the prospect starts talking about pricing or timelines, or process of change, without hearing the full story. Yes, in theory, all buying signals. But in my experience, it usually comes out as "I've heard enough. So what's it cost?" (which I interpret as "I haven't really been paying full attention, and I gave you this meeting as a courtesy. Tell me the end numbers so I can politely tell you no"). It reminds me of the guy in a restaurant not listening to the server list the specials for the evening because he's too busy looking for the meatloaf on the menu. The meatloaf is not on the menu. It was one of the specials!

Every buyer is different. I mentioned type "A" personalities earlier. Some buyers cut to the chase. Others love detailed meetings and ask lots of questions. Know your buyer. Remember, it can help you know how to close. But if negotiating breaks in during the presentation, and not always about price, learn to table it. Hold that potential piece of negotiation to the side.

For example, prospect says, "We wouldn't use three of those because we would only use one. What does that look like?" You would then come back to the prospect with the hold. "You make a good point. Putting in the services that make the most sense for you is what this meeting is all about. I've noted that. Let's set that aside and revisit it at the conclusion."

Negotiating is applying pressure to the other party. The "table-it" method works well, again, with the certain type of buyer. Depending on the buyer, I would use the value of open-ended questions to delve a little deeper into what he may have said. Maybe he is thinking through the process with me! "How do you go about the distribution currently? How might three as opposed to one benefit you?" Isn't overcoming objections a little like negotiating? Be careful in the rare instance that true negotiation starts during your presentation. It is quite hard to fully negotiate, half the picture."

Most negotiation happens at the *end* of the presentation. The prospect says she's liked what she heard, and now it's time to strike the deal. It always goes back to the presentation, doesn't it? If you asked good questions, listened well to her answers, moved her from indefinite need to definite need, intrigued a sense of urgency, trial closed along the way, your chances of her paying the cost is working more in your favor. So nearing the *end* of your presentation, when the buying signal is asked ("So how much does this cost?") you can start an assumptive close with this amazing phrase: "Well, here's the best part about it..."

Chapter 10

The Confidence in Closing

"Coffee is for closers." This is one of the all-time classic movie lines. It comes from the aforementioned 1992 film, *Glengarry Glen Ross.* This part of the film covers two days in the lives of real-estate sales representatives and the extreme measures they take to keep their jobs when the corporate office sends a sales trainer to try and motivate them. His "motivational" techniques are more threatening and demeaning.

His overall message is that within a week, all will be fired except the top two salesmen. Yikes. If that didn't put the fear in them, what would? During the trainer's "motivational tirade," one of the salesmen gets up to get coffee. The trainer basically derides him to not get any coffee because "coffee is for closers." This classic sales movie, although quite painful to watch, has another poignant sales lesson.

As I've discussed in previous chapters, the closing of the sales process really doesn't come at the end of the sales call. It's done throughout the sales call. From quality suspects, to qualifying prospects, asking good questions to maintain control, moving one from indefinite need to definite need, trial closing along the way—this is how closing is done best. Also, one doesn't have to be the world's greatest closer if she consistently does the necessary *activity* to put herself in front of enough prospects.

It's actually quite simple math. If your goal is three new deals a month and you only get in front of three decision makers a month, then you better be a *stellar* closer. If you need three new deals a month and you get in front of eight decision makers a month, then you can be a *good* closer and maybe get four or five deals that month! It always seems to go back to the activity you do, doesn't it?

That being said, we still have to *close* the deal.

In sitting through hundreds of presentations, I have found that, more often than not, the sales person attempts a "softer" close, or no close at all! I have watched many actually wait for the potential buyer to say something like, "So how do I do this?" What's extra painful is that question never coming out of the buyer's mouth! Excruciating.

It's one of the moments in the sales process where I've watched the rep do a fairly smooth presentation and then become almost undone trying to scramble at the end for how to lock it in. This once professional, competent sales person looks like a totally different person; searching for what to, say, seemingly unprepared, lost. All that "cool" they exuded during the presentation has abandoned them in the final moment of truth! Have you ever been there?

Well, that's the worst of the worst. Some manage to get to the close but choose the softer route. The two main soft closes are the famous "puppy dog close" and one I call the "the synopsis close."

The Puppy Dog Close

A family is talking about getting a dog. There is nothing wrong or urgent with having discussions with your spouse or kids about getting a dog. You outweigh the pros and the cons of what a dog would mean to the family, the investments you make both financially and time spent training, and living with a new dog.

Have you ever made the "mistake" of going to the Humane Society to just look at some dogs to help make your decision? Or have you walked into a pet store just to see what's available? And there he is—the cutest little puppy you've ever laid your eyes on. And worse, he's looking at you, seemingly saying, "Please take me home. I'll be your very best friend!" It's actually more penitent at the pound.

That sweet little dog that someone else abandoned or abused is there in a cage, hoping just to get out and be loved by a family. I'll bet there's a 90 percent chance one of those dogs is coming home with you. It's always pitched to you as a trial, but once Benji enters the home, I'll bet he's there to stay!

Why do car salespeople want you to take a test drive? When you get in that brand-new car with that new car smell, it sure beats what you're driving now and can help you move closer to driving off the lot with that brand-new car! The puppy dog close!

It's no different on a sales call. Try it out for a few weeks! We won't charge you for the first month! "Test" the equipment and compare it to what you have now and see if it is easier, faster, or more convenient. Some desperate salespeople *cut their own commission* as a form of the puppy dog close. "I'll waive this or that if you sign up today." (I would argue, if they had done more activity, they wouldn't be in this position in the first place!)

So is there anything wrong with the puppy dog close? There is one major "pro" and two major "cons." The good thing is your buyer is trying it out. If your product or service rises to the occasion, your chances are good that they keep it! The bad things are they decide it isn't better and give it back, and you are left in limbo of either that happening or your sales cycle becomes longer.

For example, what if you need this deal to hit your goals at the end of the month to maximize your commissions, and the "trial" runs into the next month or, worse, comes off the board? How are you managing multiple trials? How do you compensate for the loss? What are the potential risks of the buyer telling other potential buyers that he tried it, and it wasn't what he expected? This is now a lost referral source. The PDC can be effective when used in the right situations but is a softer sell. Softer sales are not guaranteed and may take longer.

The Synopsis Close

As a speech major from Stetson University in Deland, Florida, the first day of Speech I class, my professor stood up and said, "I want to give you the golden rule of public speaking: "*Tell them what you're going to say, tell them, and then tell them what you said.*" This reminds me of the "the Synopsis Close." This type of closing is basically akin to giving a final pitch in the form of a recap or summary.

You've told them in the appointment process why you are wanting to meet. (*Tell them what you're going to say.*) You've moved through the appointment, trying to develop a need from the buyer. The buyer has asked good questions. You've answered them superbly. (*You've told them.*) You then close by summarizing all the benefits your product or service does to enhance what you've uncovered during your need's assessment discussion. (*You tell them what you've said.*)

Your synopsis includes all the advantages and improvements that can be brought to their current situation. It's like a final pitch or commercial. And then you wait, like looking at your boss having just pitched a new idea and waiting for her response. Therein lies a bit of a problem. The synopsis close works best when the rep *includes* some sort of a request for action at the end of the synopsis! "So do you think this is something that you should take advantage of today?" Sadly, many do not add that crucial line. They finish the pitch and wait.

Sales is much about keeping control of the conversation. *You ask them*; don't wait for them to ask you! Both of these closes are good for certain situations. I have used them both, off and on, in my career.

As I stated, the puppy dog close fits a certain type of buyer. My only two negative takeaways are, first, it can slow your sales cycle down a bit. The buyer uses the product or services for some amount of time before making a full commitment to you. So you're still in limbo. Second, the temptation to waive certain fees or, worse, cut commission opportunities to sweeten the deal typically happen in this closing situation. Why give away your money?

How hard have you been pounding the phones, beating the streets, researching for hours for new leads, developing COIs, asking and searching for referrals, speaking at association meetings, closing other deals, keeping your mangers happy, sending hundreds of emails and mail outs, and wading through all the "No!" to finally get to the closing moment with someone? Frankly, you deserve the fruits of your labor! Don't give anything away.

If this buyer doesn't want to pay the price, then fundamentally she simply isn't sold. So you can resolve yourself to do two things:

work harder on your presentation to get the buy-in *throughout* your presentation and find another prospect.

The synopsis close works well *if* you have done a thorough presentation and moved the buyer from indefinite need to definite need, and you have utilized several trial closes during your appointment. Then, in theory, it's almost a no-brainer for the buyer to say yes and actually would feel odd for everyone involved for the buyer to say no.

My only word of caution is that the synopsis close is only effective if the appointment is a good two-way conversation between the sales person and the potential prospect. There must be good interaction, and the appointment is a dialogue foremost, not a monologued presentation by the sales representative. The synopsis at the end is redundant. Indefinite need *has* to have given way to definite need. Think of it like this, the buyer has followed you "down a path." The buyer has asked you questions along the way to learn more about the end destination. And when you get to the door of the destination, you stop to tell the buyer all of what you've told him is behind the door. So now the last question for the buyer is: Do you want to go through the door?

My favorite type of close is the assumptive close. There's an old sales adage that says, "Don't use the assumptive close because you will come across as the first three letters of 'assumptive.'" Obviously, I would disagree. I would say that there is legitimately a fine line. For example, there *is* a fine line between aggressive and assertive. Aggressive is the negative; assertive is the positive. (I will note the irony that the first three letters of assertive is the same as assumptive.)

I think you would agree that mostly everyone despises the "pushy" salesperson. I think, personally, that a sales person becomes "pushy" when they haven't put in the activity. They come to the end of the month or quarter and they are a few short of their goals, and they end up pressuring those last few that might get them over the finish line. I would argue, if they had spent the time developing as many new possible prospects as they could, they wouldn't be in the position to have to pressure anyone in the first place. A "pressure" sales person is probably a lazy sales person. The assumptive close is not used as a tool to be "pushy"; it is more of a tool of confidence.

The Assumptive Close

Why is it called "assumptive?" This close works best when you, the seller, get signals from the buyer throughout your meeting that he or she is believing or subscribing to what you are proposing. This is sometimes tricky as I have seen lots of salespeople miss these signals, which is bad of course. Worse, they *think* they are seeing these signals, and it's a mistake to go on and try to assume the buyer is in for the deal. Naturally, I will direct your attention back to the previous chapters that discuss the importance of developing appropriate need, asking good need-finding questions, keeping the buyer engaged in the conversation, and trial closing along the way.

Above and beyond that, pay *close* attention to your prospect. What are they doing during the meeting as far as body language? Are they physically engaged? Are their arms crossed? Are they leaning forward? Do they "feel" absorbed? Are they at least smiling? Take note of those nonverbal signals that can verify where their posture may be throughout.

Speaking of engaged, what kind of questions are they asking you? Are they superficial in nature? Or do they ask a question to explore a deeper understanding of something you said or presented? Are the questions positive in nature or more skeptical? If they ask something like, "How long does this take to implement?" Do you think that's a good sign? It is. Get your assumptive close dusted off because you may be using it in a few minutes. Or maybe they choose to make positive comments about something you've said or shown. Keep a mental note. All these are adding up to assumptive close time.

Lastly, the lack of many objections is a clear signal that you may have something. If they aren't giving you objections *and* you have several of the other signals mentioned above present, I would suggest you move right into the assumptive close. Trust me, when time comes to sign the deal, if there are any real objections, they might appear then. This could be the buyer's own protective mechanism flaring up before she officially signs the deal. But putting that objection promptly to bed should be the last hurdle.

The assumptive close just feels so good coming out of your mouth. "So when would you like to start the service?" "How many of the products do you need?" "Which location should we start with?" "When and how do you want to roll this program out?" "I'm excited you are going to join my list of happy clients. Here is the paperwork to get things underway." Assumptive closing. It doesn't get any better than this.

There are several ways to close a sale. I do not aspire to say one is better than any other.

The fact is, it depends mostly to the type of individual or individuals to whom you are presenting. You should become familiar with any and all types of closes. There are soft closes and hard closes. They come in all sorts of forms and names.

Ever heard of the thermometer close? There is one called that. Sharp angle close? You may use this without knowing what the name is! ("I will give you the extra month supply. Will you sign the contract today?") Know your audience. Many owners and executives are heavy "type-A" personalities. They don't mind the direct hard close. Others are put off by that approach and are more likely to respond to a softer (see also "puppy dog") close. If you do your job thoroughly in the need's assessment part of the presentation, trial close along the way, watch their body language, listen carefully to the questions they ask, and identify a lack of any real objections, then pull out your pen or your device, and get that newest client on the books.

Chapter 11

The Pipeline and Sales Cycle

Sales, in my opinion, is not an easy job. I think many non-salespeople have a perception that it is. It's glamorous—jumping in your nice car, running across town, having a big fancy presentation, and contracts being signed left and right. Maybe you're the sales person that flies into different cities, flying first class of course, staying at marquee hotels, taking prospects to dinners or golf outings, and having the deals closed by dessert or by the eighteenth hole. Piece of cake.

Yes, the perception of sales is often skewed. Being fair to the argument, it is also a job that can make you very successful. You can do and have a lot of the things you desire with a successful career in sales. What's wrong with that? A hard-working sales person can enjoy a very good living and career.

Over the years, in my classes, I've asked the participants to name a type of career. It was one of my early icebreakers I would use here and there. But it was also used to make a veiled point. Each of the participants would name a career choice, and the answers would be ones like doctor, lawyer, EMT, police officer, dentist, accountant, banker, etc. Remember, I am asking *salespeople* to name a job type. Ninety percent of the time, twenty people giving answers, not one said "*sales representative*," which is what *their* job was! Why?

I would need the sales psychiatrist to help define the "why." I took it as they didn't consider it a real job; or maybe, a lasting job. Sales can be very tumultuous, especially if you are not performing. It never failed to surprise me that no one would mention it. If they weren't thinking of it as a career or as their profession, would that point to a lack of confidence or success? Imagine me asking twenty chiropractors to name a profession and *not one* saying chiropractor!

Whatever their reasoning, it taught me to be even more steadfast at helping that particular class be even more successful. I am always encouraging in my classes, but when I ran into these groups, I tried to really pour on the inspiration. As I said, sales is not the easiest. I do believe, with all my heart, that it is one of the most rewarding. Not because of big commissions, those are great, but to be in a position where you can enhance the quality of one's business or help out an individual client to grow more, experience more, achieve more—the trickle-down effect is where it's at. Let me give you one example.

Several years ago, I was working with a group in Denver, Colorado. One of my participants was a young lady named Julie. After the session, she was very kind to come up to me and tell me how much the session meant to her. She was excited to use the new skills she had learned. She also said that two of her branch associates were attending tomorrow's session and was going to tell them how good it was. I thanked her for the kind words and that I would take good care of her friends tomorrow. The next day's session went well, and I got to meet Julie's partners.

My travels took me on to other cities each week, and time passed. About two years later, I was back in Denver, working for that client, and Julie met me in the room that I was going to be doing the training! She had been promoted and was now overseeing the ten or twelve branches in her area. She was the one who had put this particular training together, for she wanted all her teams to go through it.

As is custom, before I start the training, there is usually someone from the line, in this case Julie, to kick off the day. I had no idea what she was going to say. She started the meeting by telling the team that she went through this training roughly two years ago. It changed her business "life."

Her branch at the time was in consideration to close because of the lack of performance and growth of the branch. She said that after she and the other two teammates came back from my training, they committed anew. To *their* credit, not mine, they turned it around. The branch was revitalized and grew rapidly! So well, in fact, Ms.

Julie got a much-deserved promotion. She directly credited her success back to my training.

As soon as I could get up to speak, I wanted to let the class know that what I did was only about 10 percent of Julie's success story. Sure, I gave them the tools to be successful. You can give someone a lawn mower, but they then have to start it up and get busy mowing. Julie took what she received and then put it into *immediate and diligent* practice. Julie is the one who earned that promotion and enjoyed the fruits of her labor. I didn't do much at all.

Listening to her story as she told the group, I wasn't thinking of my paycheck. I was thinking, *Wow, here is the real reason I do this.* If I can, in some small way, help people, that's really what it's all about.

I want to give you some advice that you can use immediately and do diligently. Two main things that can increase your productivity and efficiency are understanding your pipeline and working on shortening your sales cycle. I briefly mentioned the sales pipeline or funnel in chapter 3. Let's take a deeper dive.

The Pipeline of Utopia

In the perfect world, you pick up the phone and call a business. The gatekeeper is the nicest gatekeeper on the planet. He lets you know the decision maker is standing right beside him and would love to take your call. The decision maker is so glad you thought of her and would love to set an appointment with you. When the appointment time rolls around, she is there and prepared to experience your excellent selling skills. After the meeting, she thinks that what you are offering is a no-brainer to add to her business. Where are all the contracts? She wants to sign them and give you all the necessary information you need so that she can start taking advantage of your products or services as soon as possible.

Lastly, she gives you the names of three other people to call on and have you use her as a reference! Wow! That was easy! Yes, it was. Too easy. In fact, that scenario may happen once out of hundreds.

This is what the utopian funnel looks like:

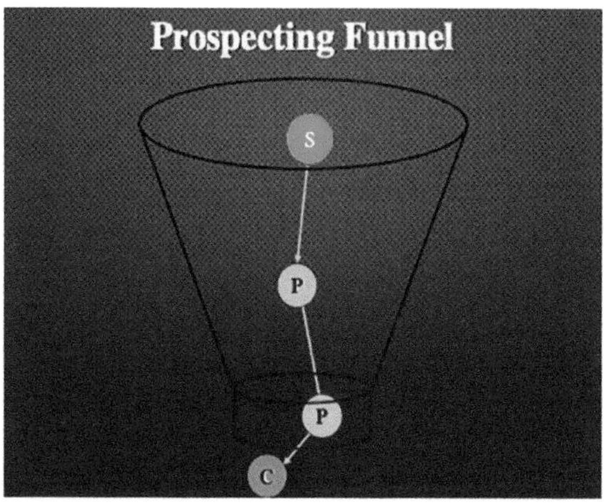

The Funnel of Reality

In the real sales world, you spend a bunch of time calling dozens of prospects. Most of them (66 percent) are unavailable to speak to you. You struggle getting an ally relationship with the gatekeeper. A few decision makers listen to your pitch for just the appointment, and the majority of them turn you down. The ones that agree sometimes pull "no-shows" or meet with you but decide not to go forward. A limited number decide to go ahead and move forward.

Here is what the funnel of reality looks like:

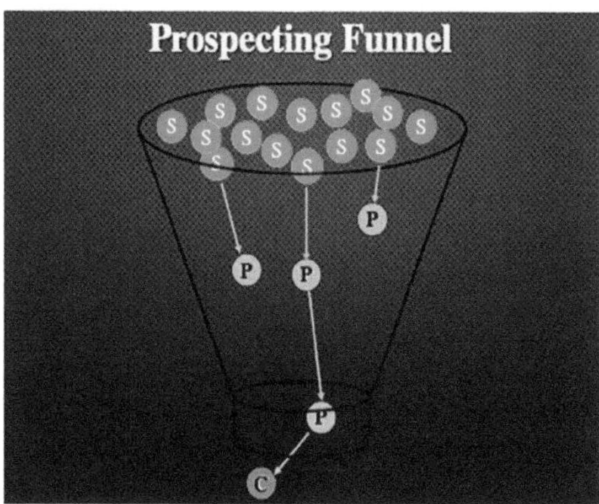

Let's explore the reality of the funnel even farther. Initially, in your training as a new sales representative, you're taught to really fill your funnel or pipeline. Good! Some prospects agree to the meetings; some don't. Some have the meetings with you and decide to move forward; some don't and decides to delay the decisions even longer.

So the middle of the funnel is where you spend a lot of your time. And rightly so! It takes a lot of work to move these suspects to prospects. It takes time to have the meetings, getting the contracts signed and moved through the proper channels for approval, gathering the information from the prospects, and negotiating the deals to completion.

As you well know, not all of them are going to buy what you have. So some prospects take almost an equal amount of time and effort only not to make it to the finish line. They determine they don't have a need, or you can't come to terms. Maybe they can't qualify for the product or services or, worse, shop you around to other competitors to have them beat your deal.

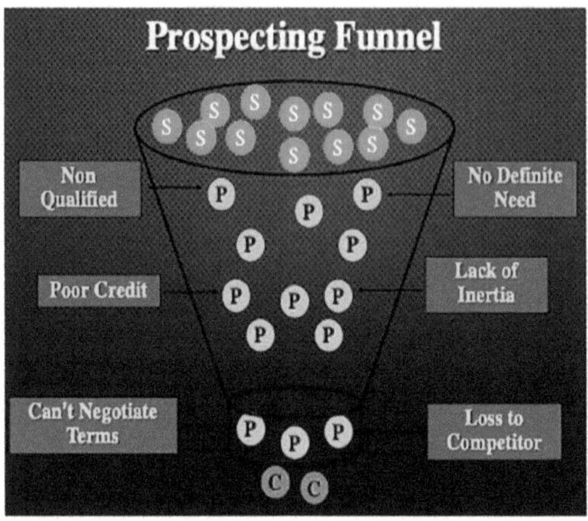

The middle of the funnel is also where you make your money! So the time and energy invested to close as many of the prospects as you can is of major importance to you. No one would complain however much time you spent if the deals come through! That isn't even the slightest problem. Still, here is where many sales representatives make a critical mistake. They spend all this time in the middle of the funnel, trying to make it happen, and what do they neglect?

They forget to do what got them there. Feed the funnel. I have heard hundreds of excuses about why they didn't feed it. The common defense is, "I was just so busy this month closing all my deals." Ah yes, the month right after the "busy" month—usually the worst month of a sales professional.

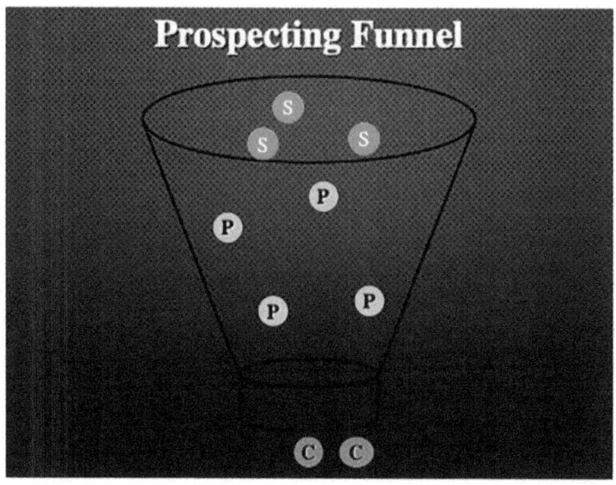

See the funnel above? All that work closing the deal left you with nothing to continue excelling. A classic mistake that many salespeople make is they do not continue the prospecting piece. Regardless of how busy you are or how idle you are, you must continue to put new prospects (or clients) into the funnel! So what is a solution?

Here is my advice: Make appointments to make appointments. Do not *find* the time; *make* the time! At the very start of each sales week, get your calendar out and book an appointment each day to do nothing but prospect for new business. Treat it as a real appointment. No interruptions, no distractions, just plan it.

I would suggest about a thirty-to-forty minute window each day of the week to prospect. This will make sure that the funnel doesn't "dry up." Yes, when you get busy, this gets harder. However, it is vital to continued success. Think of it almost like a pet. What if you didn't feed your dog for two or three days? I can't imagine he or she would be pleased with you! That's why you need to discipline yourself to do the work that gets you to where you can close a deal in the first place. Nothing happens until there is an appointment.

Back in the day, I remember a sales rep at TeleCheck named Mark in Los Angeles. He was a machine. He won the top awards every year. I imagine he had a pretty healthy paycheck too. I asked him once what's the "secret" to his success was? He said, "I never stop looking for the next customer."

For the ten years I was at TeleCheck, he was either number 1 or 2, but never out of the top 5 *every* year. Oh, and there were about 1,800 sales reps. Feed the funnel. Religiously. It will never do you any harm and will only bring and increase your success. One last thing about the funnel or pipeline as it were. Here is a little exercise you can do that can help ease a little of the pressure we are all under in sales. Learn how long your sales cycle is.

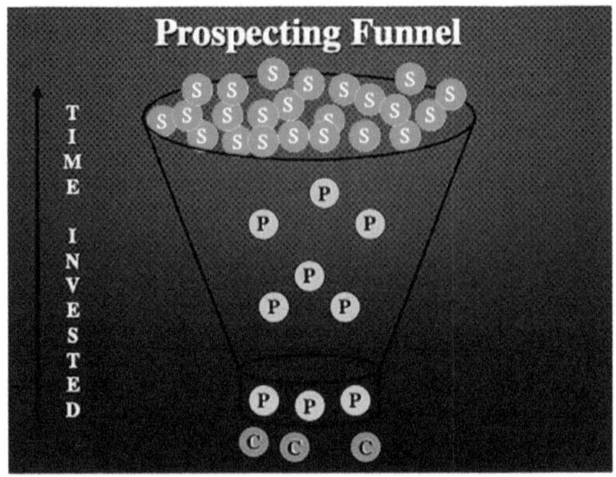

From the moment you pick up the phone to try and set an appointment with a decision maker or client, until the deal is closed, how long does that take on average? Is it a couple of days? A couple of weeks? Months? Whatever it is, learn it and know it. Why, you ask?

It's all about lowering your stress, especially toward the achievement of your goals.

If you know your sales cycle averages two weeks, when you get an appointment with a client or decision maker, if all goes as planned, you can count on it showing up for your goals in about two weeks. So now it all goes back to the activity. I know, not shocking, right?

The prospecting you do on September 1 is going to spawn some results around September 15. The prospecting you do *not* do on September 1 is not coming to see you around September 15. You can start to expect what fruits of your labor will come to pass if you've done the labor! And if you're sales cycle is longer than shorter, there's no real way to "make it up" near the end of the month or quarter!

So to compensate, do it every day! It will be challenging at first, but if you stick to it and make it a routine, you will enjoy the more success from which you've worked so hard. This isn't easy stuff! Yet, it is "doable" stuff! Feed the funnel every day. Make the time to make appointments for yourself. Stay consistent. Enjoy the results.

Chapter 12

The "Luck" Philosophy

On one of my occasions out in the field with a sales representative, we experienced the epitome of what many sales reps call "luck." It had already been a long day. It was one of those "good" long days because we had been busy. This particular sales person was quite sharp. Her name was Allison. Allison had been with the company in Dallas, Texas, for about two years and was already one of the consistent top producers.

As you know, when I would go out to work in the field with our reps, it was pretty much expected for the rep to have some appointments scheduled. This way, I could watch and coach them where I could. I was tasked to help them mostly with their presentations. Are they asking good questions, developing need, or doing good demos? Are they holding firm to their pricing? Are they not giving away their commissions unnecessarily?

Allison was pretty much excellent at all of it. On this day, we had four back-to-back appointments. The only stress we had was making sure we could make it to the next appointment. That's my kind of stress! It was somewhere around 4:00 p.m. when we finished the last appointment and had about a forty-five-minute drive back to the office. Allison mentioned that there was an area on the way back that she hadn't spent much time prospecting and asked if we could swing by. Impressed with her dedication, I said, "Let's do it!"

The "area" was an industrial park. It had maybe eight to ten businesses in it. We decided to start at one end and walk in on each and every one of them. The very last business on the park was strange.

First of all, there was no signage. All the windows were tinted black. So were the front glass doors. Allison and I looked at each other, and she wondered to me whether we should go in or not? I had a little hesitation myself. What was behind the door? What were we walking into? All sorts of bad possibilities began filling my mind. However, the curiosity in me prevailed, and I told her that it might go south or it might be a nice surprise. So we opened the door.

To say that I was immediately relieved would be an understatement. The door opened up to a very nice lobby. It looked like a very professional establishment. Across the way was a young lady sitting at what looked to be a reception desk. Allison and I went over to her and started a conversation about meeting the owner, and we asked what exactly they did here?

It turned out that it was one of the country's largest magician supply companies. They shipped magic supplies to magicians all over the world. A magician needs his or her cape and top hat and all of the other trick supplies to be the best magician he or she can be!

This particular company was not open to the public. No need for a sign. So we asked to speak to the owner. The owner happened to be there. He was a former magician who started this business years ago and it was amazingly successful. He even did a couple of magic tricks for us much to our delight.

In our need's assessment, he identified one of the frustrations was a large portion of his business was COD (cash on delivery.) The main challenge was when he received an order, he would have to wait days, and if internationally, weeks for the checks to clear before he could send the materials out. The consequence was many of his clients were frustrated with how long it took to get their supplies and looking elsewhere for faster service. When we told him that we specialize in approving those COD checks instantly and that he would have the confidence to go ahead and ship immediately, he was all about signing up to get it going.

Allison gave him all the pricing and contracts, and he signed them on the spot. He became one of the biggest clients in Allison's area as far as revenue, and she made a nice commission for her efforts. It was magic! As we left the business and headed back to the office,

Allison asked, "How lucky was that?" Thank goodness I had the sense enough to explain to her that it wasn't luck at all. I said to her, "Do you remember after the last appointment we had earlier in the day, telling me there was a place you hadn't spent any time prospecting and would I mind if we could swing by? The minute you made that decision, you just cancelled the 'luck' part of it. You chose to go to this industrial park. You chose to walk in on each and every one of them. You chose to go into a no-sign having, dark-window tinted scary-looking business. What was lucky about that?" It taught Allison and refreshed me to remember something: the harder you work, the "luckier" you get.

If you feel a common theme throughout this book, it is done with complete intent. It really is a simple requisite. The more activity you do, proactively, the more successful you are going to be. I work with salespeople all the time, and it might not surprise you how much of the "coming-to-you" business they work versus the "going-and-get" business. They seem to only want the leads and referrals and hope that it puts them over the finish line each month or quarter. And they always seemed to be stressed, right? Where are the salespeople like Allison or Mark? Dare I say that for some, it may be lazy? At least Ricky was honest enough about himself to quit and realize this wasn't the job for him.

I had a sales representative in my days as district manager in the Carolinas who had been working for a long time in the area. She knew everyone. She worked the greater Charlotte area. Lots of businesses to work. She relied on her referrals only. She only wanted to work the "bigger" deals. None of these, standing on their own, is wrong. However, there were months where the easy leads were few, and the once gigantic referral sources ran dry. She would struggle. Because of her strategy, she all but forgot the hard work to put out there calling on any and all she could. She usually was on top of the "leader board."

Along comes another sales rep who had a smaller area without the big city of Charlotte. She was a bulldog! She was tough and gritty and not a fear in her body to get out there and work hard. In just a short time, the torch was passed. There was a new number 1. There was no luck involved in this process, just the conscious decision to go out there and search for it. The hunter. I wonder sometimes if the hunter is a dying breed? I sure hope not.

By far, the best salespeople I have been around are the hunters. They are constantly looking for new business. If you live long enough in sales, you hear or develop your own excuses. The irony is, there is no excuse not to look for new business. Always try to keep yourself proactive not reactive. Anything you get reactively is a bonus! Where you really become successful is in your proactivity. Where you really get "lucky" is what you choose to do as far as your activity. So how is it best to do this?

Discipline Yourself

Many salespeople, as a rule, are not a disciplined group. They are outgoing, people-friendly, and juggle a lot of balls in the air. They drop everything and chase the next lead that looks more promising and forget about some of the others that are just as close. The first thing to do is get organized. It's hard. I know from firsthand experience! If you invest the time to organize yourself, you can stay more focused on the task at hand and not wander off into the "jungle" of other areas. Stay resolute to what is before you and try not to deviate until the task is complete.

Eliminate Distractions

Put yourself in an environment that can help you excel. With clients walking up on you, emails popping left and right, your cell phone asking you to check the latest results from your Fantasy Football League, and your fellow associates bothering you (what's the first three letters of "associate"?), it probably isn't conducive to an effective day. Find a quiet distraction free zone to maximize the task at hand. I never make outbound cold calls to new businesses in the middle of the floor in my office. How can I concentrate and successfully navigate the gatekeeper dilemma and then handle the owner, if I get her, with the commotion of the office running rampant?

Set Reasonable Goals

Change doesn't normally happen overnight. Set goals for yourself and make them reasonable. I hear salespeople say things like, "I'm not going to stop calling until I get ten appointments!" Well, go home and bring an air mattress back with you. On a flat cold call, the average success rate given for an appointment is 5 percent (with no training) and with 66 percent of decision makers unavailable to speak with you, you would need to make roughly six hundred phone calls to get ten appointments; with good training, you might be able to pull it off with ninety to one hundred calls.

Who's reading this sentence wants to make between one hundred to six hundred calls *per day*? The goal itself is unrealistic. Ninety calls a day is a different goal than ninety calls a week! I have met many a manager who made the mistake of expecting unrealistic goals to be met. I understand that they have bosses pressuring them to get their teams to achieve, but the goal has to be practical. You're not going to change the way you've been doing things tomorrow.

Start setting small goals throughout your work week that you can achieve to maximize your activity. As you start to consistently meet those goals, bump them up. For example, I'm honest with myself that I haven't been asking for referrals after any of my meetings because I'm uncomfortable doing so. This week, my goal is to ask for five referrals. Not get! Ask!

If you average two meetings per day and set the goal of five, then you just did it in half of your meetings. This is way better than the previous *none.* Set realistic expectations for yourself. Take one step out of your "norm" and then move it to two steps and so on. Unrealistic goals are demotivational. Reasonable goals spur confidence and success.

Create a Schedule

Remember, I suggested to "make appointments to make appointments"? How about setting a schedule for your whole day or week? Block out areas of times to work on the specific tasks you need to undertake. When you are in these blocks, you focus only on the mission for that expanse. Sure, in sales, at any time, your plan may need to change based on the situation. The more you stick to your calendar, the more effective and efficient you can be. You also become much more economical with your time. Here is a sample sales calendar that is heavily activity driven:

Sample Schedule To Sales Success

Week: 1/1/21 Start Time: 7:00 AM

	Mon	Tue	Wed	Thu	Fri	Sat
7:00 AM	FUEL!	FUEL!	FUEL!	FUEL!	FUEL!	
7:30 AM	FUEL!	FUEL!	FUEL!	FUEL!	Networking Meet	
8:00 AM	Develop Prospecting Lists	Outbound Calling for New Appointments	Develop Prospecting Lists	Outbound Calling for New Appointments	Develop Prospecting Lists	
8:30 AM	Develop Prospecting Lists	Outbound Calling for New Appointments	Develop Prospecting Lists	Outbound Calling for New Appointments	Develop Prospecting Lists	
9:00 AM	Follow-Ups with Recent Appointments	Reserved for New Appointments	Follow-Ups with Recent Appointments	Reserved for New Appointments	Follow-Ups with Recent Appointments	
9:30 AM	Follow-Ups with Recent Appointments	Reserved for New Appointments	Follow-Ups with Recent Appointments	Reserved for New Appointments	Follow-Ups with Recent Appointments	
10:00 AM	Propecting In-Person	Reserved for New Appointments	Follow-Ups with Recent Appointments	Reserved for New Appointments	Propecting In-Person	
10:30 AM	Propecting In-Person	Reserved for New Appointments	Propecting In-Person	Reserved for New Appointments	Propecting In-Person	
11:00 AM	Propecting In-Person	Reserved for New Appointments	Propecting In-Person	Reserved for New Appointments	Propecting In-Person	
11:30 AM	Propecting In-Person	Reserved for New Appointments	Propecting In-Person	Reserved for New Appointments	Propecting In-Person	
12:00 PM	Lunch	Lunch	Lunch	Lunch	Lunch	
12:30 PM	Outbound Calling for New Appointments	Call Existing Clients for Referrals	Outbound Calling for New Appointments	Call Existing Clients for Referrals	Outbound Calling for New Appointments	
1:00 PM	Outbound Calling for New Appointments	Office/Paperwork/COI	Outbound Calling for New Appointments	Office/Paperwork/COI	Outbound Calling for New Appointments	
1:30 PM	Reserved for New Appointments	Office/Paperwork/COI	Reserved for New Appointments	Office/Paperwork/COI	Reserved for New Appointments	
2:00 PM	Reserved for New Appointments	Follow-Ups with Recent Appointments	Reserved for New Appointments	Follow-Ups with Recent Appointments	Reserved for New Appointments	
2:30 PM	Reserved for New Appointments	Follow-Ups with Recent Appointments	Reserved for New Appointments	Follow-Ups with Recent Appointments	Reserved for New Appointments	
3:00 PM	Reserved for New Appointments	Prospecting In-Person	Reserved for New Appointments	Prospecting In-Person	Reserved for New Appointments	
3:30 PM	Reserved for New Appointments	Prospecting In-Person	Reserved for New Appointments	Prospecting In-Person	Reserved for New Appointments	
4:00 PM	Reserved for New Appointments	Prospecting In-Person	Reserved for New Appointments	Prospecting In-Person	Reserved for New Appointments	
4:30 PM	Call Existing Clients for Referrals	Prospecting In-Person	Call Existing Clients for Referrals	Prospecting In-Person	Call Existing Clients for Referrals	
5:00 PM	Office Work/Paperwork/COI	Develop Prospecting Lists	Office Work/Paperwork/COI	Develop Prospecting Lists	Office Work/Paperwork/COI	
5:30 PM	Office Work/Paperwork/COI	Develop Prospecting Lists	Office Work/Paperwork/COI	Develop Prospecting Lists	Office Work/Paperwork/COI	
6:00 PM	Association Presentation		Chamber Meeting			

Stay Consistent

The *more* you do something, the *better* you do something. The only way you enhance your skills is to practice those skills consistently. If you make enough calls to businesses, you will run into a lot of gatekeepers. If those gatekeepers always ask, "What is this regarding?" and you've learned to say, "I wanted to get his/her opinion on a couple ideas I have on improving cash flow and reduce overhead expenses. Could you put me through?" Then each time you address it, you build more confidence. You build more sureness.

The more you do presentations and attempt to move prospects from indefinite need to definite need through good question asking, the more capable you become. The additional times you stick firm on your price, the added times you get your price. When you regularly ask for referrals at the end of meetings, you move the bar from getting some to getting many. When you follow your calendar dependably, it is only going to augment your activity, which leads to more opportunity, which leads to more success. Both the *quantity* and *quality* of your production will proliferate your achievement to new summits. The best news is none of this is impossible. In fact, it's categorically viable. So get to it!

I've learned in my career that luck just doesn't exist in sales. In fact, I will tell you this: Sales success is nothing more than getting the right person, at the right time, and under the right conditions. Once you have those three things in place, you're probably about to get your next sale. It takes a lot of hard work to find the prospect that meets all three. They don't fall out of trees, and they certainly don't normally come to their own realizations and call *you*. You and I have to go find them. That demands an immense amount of good, quality, and focused activity.

You will fight through way more immediate and, even worse, delayed rejection than you will acceptance. *They just weren't the right person*. You will hear over and over that they need to think about it or talk it over with others in their organization. *The timing is not right.* You will get told that they don't want to or can't do this for a number of different reasons. *They aren't under the right conditions.* So what is our only solution? To quit? To try something else? To complain to our peers or managers? The buyer is uncontrollable. However, your activity is. I will promise you this: the more activity you do, the harder you work, the more skilled you become, the "luckier" you will get.

Chapter 13

The Twenty-Eight Years of Questions

There's an old expression that reads, "I've seen it all." I can't say that I have literally seen it all, but I will tell you that I have seen a lot. I have had the pleasure of cold-calling in Hawaii, which is an oxymoronic statement. I have cold-called in a place called Duluth, Minnesota, which would not be an expression with contradictory words. I have worked in all fifty states. The last one to complete the list was Montana in 2018. I've worked in many parts of Canada, an amazingly beautiful country. I've traveled up and down the streets of Old San Juan in Puerto Rico. It's been an amazing journey so far. The sights and sounds I've had the privilege to experience has been one of the greatest perks of the job.

More importantly are the thousands of people I have had the honor to meet and work for and with. I have worked for some of the best people in the business. I have had mentors throughout my career who have looked after me and guided me. They have counseled me, corrected me, and uplifted me. They encouraged me in the good times, and in some of the times, I felt I wasn't doing the best that I thought I could. Many of them and I still communicate to this very day. All of you know who you are, and I can't thank each of you enough.

The greatest joy of my "career" is the thousands of salespeople I have had the honor of working with. I have met with some of the nicest, craziest, kindest, strangest, hardest-working, laziest, honest, insincere, unique, and special sales representatives. Each and every one of them taught me something. I think I learned more from them than they ever learned from me. In their own individual way, they contributed to where I am today. For that, I am deeply grateful.

It has been something of a wild ride. I'll never forget meeting the rep in Manhattan, who was wearing a fedora and a long coat, ready to cold-call. He even had a walking cane! And he was a young guy! He was wonderfully loud and full of life, and I loved every minute with him!

There was a rep, originally from Jamaica, who took me cold calling in Washington Heights. I don't think that particular area of Manhattan in the early 1990s was used to two men in suits walking into their business unexpectedly. We walked into one that day, and the only three people in the store dropped everything and ran out the back door! Why? To this day, I don't know!

Once, I was talking to an owner just outside of her dry-cleaning business in Jacksonville, Florida. The rep who was with me, Tangee, reached out and slapped my cheek in mid-sentence. For a moment, I panicked that I had said something terribly wrong and just froze. Thankfully, it was just that a mosquito had landed on my face, and she was just trying to rid me of it. When we finally got back in the car and drove away, we started laughing so hard that we had to pull the car over to catch our breath. Seriously.

I had a representative in Los Angeles that took me to an appointment but didn't want to tell me what it was. I quickly realized why when we entered the giant warehouse of a large adult-video distribution center. Before I could get us out of there, the owner came up and started to talk to us. Imagine the stereotype, and you get the picture. I could go on and on.

I remember my very first sale. It was for a trucking company in Orlando. I remember worrying if I were saying the right things, demoing the right way, and getting all the paperwork filled out correctly. I can still recall those nerves running through my body. It also didn't help that there were four decision makers in the meeting with me. I was brand-new and hadn't gotten a firm grasp of everything yet.

I remember saying, "That's a good question. I can get you the answer to that." For whatever reason, they moved on to closing the deal and became a happy client of mine for many years. I also remember the first bank I ever sold: AmSouth Bank. I had prospected the chief retail officer for almost two years. We played "cat and mouse" for what seemed like an eternity. I had the right *person*, but I didn't have the right *time* and *conditions* lining up.

One day, almost 730 days later, I called and got the CRO on the phone. After pleasantries and asking again if now may be the time, he said to me, "Chris, if you can teach our people to be as persistent as you are, maybe we should finally take a look at it."

Soon after, John Gehegan and I were on a plane to Birmingham, Alabama. We closed the deal, and AmSouth became a very good client. After a few years, they were acquired by Regions Bank. We were in limbo as to whether Regions would keep us after the acquisition. We came to learn that Regions only kept two vendors from the AmSouth side, and we were one of the two! Regions and our firm still share a great relationship after almost fifteen-plus years. Yes, I can honestly say the years I've been selling and training have been amazing. I have enjoyed each step of the way.

Over these great number of years, I've been asked lots of sales questions. I don't know that I've had the perfect answers but thought I would give you some of the most asked questions and, at least, my opinion of the answers to them.

Should I always confirm the appointments I make?

Manny reps ponder this question. Some reps think they should for various reasons, and some think they shouldn't mainly because it gives the other person the opportunity to easier get out of it. In my view, the rule of confirming appointments goes like this: *If they are coming to see you, always confirm. If you're going to see them, never confirm.* Understanding that "always" and "never" are not absolutes; this is the general rule.

If the prospect or client is coming to your appointment at your office or some other designated meeting place, then the best practice is to confirm this meeting at least by the day before the meeting. Why? Your time is also as valuable as their time! You have built a schedule to keep your activity thriving, and this is an allocated part of that schedule to run appointments.

If the prospect or client pulls a "no-show," you can waste valuable time waiting for someone who isn't going to be there. Wouldn't you rather know beforehand instead of sitting there waiting for something that isn't going to happen? Not only does it waste time, but it also puts a damper on your attitude. The dejection of something you hoped for and was looking forward to can linger for a while. You wasted time and energy on something that you couldn't control. If you reach out to confirm and find it isn't going to happen earlier than later, maybe there's time to fill that new open spot! Think of it now as a new challenge. Who can I get to replace what I have lost? Go for it! You c*A*n do it some of the time, and that brings a *C*ertain amount of *T*riumph.

If you are going to see a prospect or client at their place of business or designated spot, never confirm. Let me clarify the absolute on this one by giving you two exceptions to the rule. The only time I confirm the appointment of someone I am going to see revolves around *distance* in time or geography. If I have scheduled an appointment out in *time*, like a month from now, I will usually call to confirm because we set the appointment several days or weeks ago. If I have a scheduled appointment where the distance is great and would have to drive an hour or more, then I would probably confirm before I made the trip.

If my appointment is local, I never call to confirm the meeting. Why? I mentioned this in a previous chapter, but just to refresh, there are three scenarios when you show up for an appointment. First, the person is there, and you have a good meeting. Second, the person pulls a "no-show." Third, the person is there, but the meeting is over quickly because there was no present need. As usual, the activity handles any and all scenarios.

Let's look at scenario no. 1. You and your prospect or client have a good appointment. It lasts your normal thirty to forty-five minutes, and you finish the meeting with a good feeling that this is a viable deal for you! Great! Now don't make an activity mistake! Most salespeople hop in their car and rush back to the office. Don't do it yet. While you're there in this part of the field, walk into a few businesses around where your appointment was. Try to hit three or four before you head out. Worst case, you get some new information on business owners, times available, information about the business itself. Maybe you get to meet the owner! Maybe he or she wants to talk. Of course, this is pertinent to the type of sales you are in. If what you are selling is something that can be easily presented in this context, then go for it. If you are selling to larger companies, it obviously becomes less applicable.

Scenario no. 2: the dreaded "no-show." Let's understand two types of "no-shows": legitimate and illegitimate. Sometimes, life happens, and the owner truly did not intend to blow you off. For example, a child was sick at school, an emergency at one of her other locations, or he genuinely forgot about the meeting. In other words, they *legitimately* did not try to blow you off on purpose. So first of all, they owe you; and second, most owners or decision makers with any ounce of decency would try to notify you or easily reschedule because of the inconvenience to you.

The *illegitimate* "no-show" is different. They *knowingly* blow you off. "Tell them I'm too busy to meet," they'll say. I would ask you this: Do you want this type of individual as a client? I have a word for you: *next*! Spend your quality of time with quality prospects. Regardless of the type of "no-show," do not go to your car dejected. You were going to be sitting in a meeting for thirty to forty-five minutes. Spend that time in the area you are right now! Make up for the disappointing *mistep* and *step into* as many businesses as you can. There may be that diamond in the rough or a magician's surprise waiting for you.

Lastly, the quick meeting. You have the meeting, but one or both of you realize that there just isn't a need, and it ends early. Can you now guess what you should do? That's right! Spend the rest of the time making up for lost time. It's really quite simple. Many salespeople don't do it. *You* do it, and watch the difference it makes.

Is this a sales call?

I touched on this briefly as an example in an earlier chapter. Many, if not most, salespeople squirm when they get asked this question from a suspect, prospect, or client. They call or walk into a business, and as soon as someone asks, "Is this a sales call?" they stumble and stagger through an answer. Interestingly, I ask my classes sometimes if they think the call they are making is a sales call. Would it shock you that the majority said no?

Let's break this sentence down to the core. First of all, is "Is this a sales call?" an objection or a question? Most think it's an objection, especially when they add how the people *sound* when they're saying it. The fact is, it is a question. Not an objection. Go back to third grade with me for a minute. When your sweet teacher was showing you a sentence that ended with a question mark, did she tell you that the sentence was an *objection*? *No*! She said this sentence is a question! So we are not going to handle it as an objection with a great response and a request for action. "Is this a sales call?" is a question. "I don't do sales calls" is an objection.

As we also learned earlier, there are closed-ended questions and open-ended questions. "Is this a sales call?" is a closed-ended question. So answer it closed ended with "Yes."

I've listened to sales reps answer like, "Well, it's kind of a courtesy call? I was hoping we could maybe talk about a few things and..." In sales, it's always better to answer closed-ended questions close-ended, and open-ended questions open-ended. If you can't bring yourself to answer just, "Yes" then try, "I hope so," and keep going!

Finally, the truth of the matter is it *is* a sales call. Are you not wanting them to meet to *purchase* your products and services? It has always astounded me the number of *salespeople* afraid to say they are trying to make a *sale*.

Gang, are we selling something or are we not? Here is some good news: nothing happens in business until someone sells something. Why shy away from this fact? Think about this, every business you're trying to sell to, what are *they* doing? Trying to sell something. So guess what? This *is* a sales call, you are going to love it, I'm going to make sure you need it, and I'm then expecting you to buy it!

Should I leave voice mails?

If I had a quarter for every time that I was leaving a voice mail for someone and my phone started beeping and it was the very person I was leaving a voice mail for, I could probably buy a new set of golf clubs! If I had a dollar for everyone I asked, "Did you get my message?" and they said, "No, I was just calling you back," I might be able to get tickets to The Masters.

Each company probably has a policy on whether they want their salespeople to leave messages or not. If the policy is "Yes, we want you to leave messages for contacts or prospects," fine. Leave a message. Follow the three Ps: positive, pithy, and plain. No one likes to listen to a voice mail where the speaker sounds like they would rather be anywhere but here, leaving a voice mail. People can play voice mails over and over. So when you hear the "beep," be *positive* and confident.

Next, make sure your voice mail is *pithy*. You don't want the other person zoning out during your monologue. Keep it concise and to the point. Save all the other complexities for the meeting!

Lastly, keep it *plain*. This sounds similar to pithy, but it is different. Whenever you are leaving voice mails, mostly to existing clients, there might be information that can only be disclosed to that particular account holder or client. Maybe the person answering the phone or listening to the message is not on the account of the person you need. So keep it *plain*. You can't control who has access to the message, so control what you say.

<u>Here is an example</u>: "*Hello! This message is for Jack Thompson. Jack, this is Chris Lovett, and I am with ABC Company. I have an idea I would like to run by you and get your opinion on it. Would you call me at 407-555-1212? Thanks, and have a great day.*"

What happens if you have the option not to leave a message? Then don't! I will tell you that over the last several years of my career, I have stopped leaving voice mails for people. I don't leave them for clients. I don't leave them for prospects. I don't leave them for family members! Are there exceptions to every rule? Of course. But as a rule, I don't leave voice mails unless I have to. Why?

Sixty-six percent of the people you try to reach at any given time, on any given list, for any given reason, are not available. So if I'm calling twenty prospects a day, that means I'll be leaving about thirteen messages a day. Good luck with the follow-up. For me, I try to reach a prospect a few times before I consider voice mail. Let's say, I try her at 9:00 a.m. on Monday. I may try again around 3:30 p.m. Tuesday around 11:00 a.m., then 5:30 p.m. Wednesday, right at noon. Thursday at 7:30 a.m. and 2:00 p.m. Then I may decide to leave a voice mail.

Here is an example: "*Hello, Jack. This is Chris Lovett with ABC Company. I've tried to reach you a few times in person this week. Please call me when you have a moment. 407-555-1212. Thank you!*"

As a rule, I stay away from voice mails. My one main exception is if I have a client or prospect who *asks me* to call, say, on Friday, for a follow-up. I will try that owner a few times to get with her as she asked. If I am not successful near the end of the day, I will leave a voice mail, letting her know that I tried to do what she asked me to do.

As I've gotten better with my own skills, I have learned the skill of "advancement" and now try to nail down a specific time and day to follow up. Then I can send invites to remind the client of our follow-up. Then the voice mails become even more scarce. There is really no right or wrong here. Just decide which way takes up more of your activity time and go with the other choice.

Which way is the best way to prospect?

The best way is using all the ways on a regular basis. There are no shortcuts in sales.

What is the hardest part of sales?

This is a loaded question because "sales" can be both very general and very specific.

In the broadest sense, in my opinion, getting the appointment is by far the hardest part. Here is a cold fact: You cannot sell anything to anyone until you have someone. The work it takes to first find a viable suspect, then the preparation to make good contact, then successfully navigating any admin or gatekeeper screens to get to that contact, and then to convince that person to meet and *be there* when you get there is the hardest part. Once you have earned the "yes" to the meeting, now you have someone.

Then specifically, the hardest part is working to get someone to move from indefinite need to definite need. To mature in your questioning process, to get someone to see the need or the problem, and to get them to want to do something about it is perhaps the hardest to really master. Once you do, it is a game changer. So ask more questions, listen honestly, talk when needed, and win more business.

When calling for the appointment, should I ask if this is a good time to speak?

Many people think, "No way!" You give them the opportunity to say "no," and the phone calls ends. Are they right? Well, yes. "Are you busy right now, or do you have a minute?" And then they say, "I'll let you guess." (*Click!*) Hilarious. But can I argue that they can do it even if you don't acknowledge the interruption? "Hi. This is Chris from ABC Company, and we have an amazing new service that..." (*Click!*) So whether you do or whether you don't, it still can happen.

Want to be more successful? In this case, decide what most people do, and do the opposite. I will bet that if you paid attention to the next phone calls you receive either at work, cell, or home in the ensuing twenty-four hours, you would not need more than one hand to count the number of people who ask you if it is an okay time to speak. Everyone else cuts right to the case.

Take a moment and ask the person you have just called, out of the blue and are clearly interrupting, if this is a good time to speak. It's courteous, it separates you from the pack, a better chance they are listening to you, and whatever their answer is to the question will lead you to a "green light" more often than not.

How long should I keep a prospect on my list?

Of all the questions, this one might be the hardest to answer. The end result in sales is the sale. It is extremely hard to let go of a prospect that you have worked and been inching ever so closely to a deal. "I'm going to buy it from you, I promise." Then days turn into weeks, and then to, yikes, months!

When a prospect drags on and stalls, in my opinion, it really boils down to two scenarios. One is he is so completely disorganized that he can't keep deadlines or next steps in order and struggles completing all the phases to move into the customer category or takes a painstakingly long time to do so.

The second scenario, and more likely the problem, is he isn't sold. If he were, he would have that sense of urgency I mentioned before. Remember, people buy anything because they see the need *and* want to do something about it. Sometimes, people don't like to be the bearer of bad news and have to tell you no. Or tell you, "I've changed my mind and going with someone else." So they "ghost."

Understanding that, is there still an answer to "how long?" My suggestion would be this: Use your sales cycle as a guide. What is your average sales cycle? From the minute you make first contact to that decision maker until she signs on the dotted line to be your next customer, how long does it take on average? Is it four days? Is it three weeks? Is it a month? Whatever it is, the maximum time you keep someone on your target list is three times your sales cycle. If they haven't made any major progress in that time frame, move them off the list and find another prospect. By the way, three is the maximum. If there is no real movement by the middle of two times your cycle, it probably isn't going to happen. At least for now.

What do I do when I struggle with the constant rejection?

First, understand that it's completely normal to face rejection in sales. The number 1 answer in sales is no. By a longshot, it isn't even close. The world's greatest closers may hit an overall 40 percent success rate. The rest of *us* are going to be even lower. But even the greatest still have a wide majority of no.

Second, you can always strive to improve your activity and your performance. A good start is taking the time to read this book. You should read many more sales books. We all learn from each other, and this is your career. Sometimes I think of a sales book, mine included, like the owner's manual for a car. People go out and buy a 50,000-dollar vehicle and very rarely read the owner's manual. Only when there is a problem, or something they can't figure out, do they turn to it.

What if you sat down and read through the material that explains what to do and how to best enjoy what you have dropped $50,000 on? Would it help you in the performance and features of your new car? You made a decision to start a career in sales and have goals and dreams of your own! Read all you can and learn! Improve! Practice your performance. Role-play with your spouse or your dog, whoever will listen, and work on your craft.

And lastly, don't take yourself too seriously. Have fun. Enjoy what it is that you do. Be the value they are looking for. If this particular client or prospect says no, that is okay. They are more quicker getting out of the way to the one that's going to tell you yes. And if you haven't experienced it at all yet, or even just a few times, the one that says yes and fills out all the paperwork and is excited about having what you provided has a unique way of making all those previous nos go away. Hang in there. Keep your activity *consistent*. The ones that will say yes *are* out there. We just have to go find them!

Chapter 14

The Sales Road Less Traveled

When I was young, I never had the answer to "What are you going to be when you grow up?" Even through junior high (that's middle school to most of you reading this) and high school, I never developed, I guess, what you would call my passion. I had friends who were going to the military, becoming lawyers, doctors, first responders, etc. Many of my friends knew exactly what they "wanted to be" when they grew up. I did not.

As I look back, I believe a lot of my work life was defined by chance, opportunity, and circumstance. I came from a musical family and knew enough just to keep myself entertained. But I was far from prolific. I messed around with the piano and could put a few chords together, but once I was put into piano lessons, my desire, and pretty much laziness, put that to bed.

In seventh grade, I signed up for a band and told them I was going to play the drums. That seemed pretty easy. Not long after joining the band, our band director, Denny Turner, wanted to start a jazz band. My best friend at the time was a much better drummer, so he took that. Mr. Turner came to me and said, "I'd like for you to play bass guitar." I had never held a guitar. He said that it had four strings—E, A, D, and G—and each fret was a half-step.

My limited piano training reminded me what that meant, and I figured if I wanted to be in the band, I would have to figure it out. And I did. For the next three years of junior high and the three years of high school, that core of students stuck together, and we turned out to be a pretty good jazz band. In fact, in high school, senior year, we were awarded the top jazz band in the state of Florida out of about thirty. I wasn't a fantastic bass player. I was a good utility player.

When it came time to graduate from high school, I still had no idea what I was going to do or what college I was going to attend. If I didn't have a specific career aspect in mind, it complicates what school to apply to or choose.

Many of my friends were going to this school called Stetson University. It is located in Deland, Florida—between Orlando and Daytona Beach. They had an excellent music school. So I figured I would tag along. I auditioned for a scholarship on the bass guitar and upright bass for orchestra, and somehow, they gave me a little money to help defray my expenses. So off to Stetson I went.

The whole rhythm section we had from junior high to high school were now at Stetson and stayed together for the rest of our time in college. Not knowing what I really wanted to do, I declared a music major for my degree. After about a year, I began to realize that, although I loved music, I didn't want to eat, sleep, and breathe music. So I needed to change my degree. What to? I still had no inner voice saying, "Become a psychologist!" So I switched from a music major to a BA in liberal arts with a speech and theater major. I think I chose it for the degree that required the least amount of Math!

When I finished my time at Stetson, again, like when I finished high school, I had no real direction. I was pretty sure I was not going to head to New York City or Los Angeles to become the next Tom Hanks. As I've told you before, I joined University High School as a teacher, and then went through the RIFT, and made my way to TeleCheck, then First Data, and then finally to John Gehegan and Gehegan & Associates.

Although I had no preplanned road to travel, I have made the most of the opportunities that came my way. I had never played bass before. Never acted or directed a play. I had never taught a class on anything, much less speech/debate/drama and English. I had never sold something, managed anyone, or trained anyone. Each stretch of the road, I had to learn and do.

I also happened to go down a road, sales, that is very goal-driven. A road that if you don't earn it, you don't get anything for it.

A road that is continuously filled with "what have you done for me lately?" This road has lots of stress and challenges. This road also has lots of accomplishment, achievement, joy, and reward.

The great poem, *The Road Less Traveled*, by Robert Frost ends with this:

> *Two roads diverged in a wood, and I—*
> *I took the one less traveled by,*
> *And that has made all the difference.*

His premise is there are two roads. One road is easier. It is clearer and cleaner. There are less obstacles and challenges and is the road that many or most people take. It doesn't portray to be a bad choice, for it can lead you to a certain destination that can also bring happiness and fulfillment.

The other road is less traveled by. Maybe this road has more challenges to it. Sharper turns. More impediments. It isn't as clear because it could be a little overgrown. This road will be harder. It will test your resolve. It will force you to defy its complications. And once you have persevered from the beginning to the end of this road, you will find a deeper sense of accomplishment. Your achievement might feel more complete. Your success more personally warranted.

As I see it, there are two roads that take you from start to finish though the "wood" of sales. Acknowledging that I have said that sales is not as easy a job as many people think, there is an easier road and the one less traveled by.

The easier road is to rely on referrals and rely on leads being presented to you. Take a "sales" job where there is no commission attached to it so you don't necessarily have to worry about goals. Or finally, to do the minimum duty to keep yourself as an average sales representative in good standing. By default, you are that reactive sales person more than a proactive sales person!

Don't misunderstand! You are not "bad." What you are doing isn't "wrong." You just are indirectly or directly choosing that road. *I* have also chosen that road a few times when it came to defining what I wanted to do in life!

The *harder* of the two roads through the woods of sales is the one less traveled by. Want just one of a thousand examples? Seventy-five percent of all salespeople fail to ask for a referral in any meeting. Twenty-five percent do. Those 25 percent are on the road less traveled, the harder route! This road is more difficult.

It takes more discipline, more determination, and more organization. It takes more initiative in many areas of the process to be assertive and push the boundaries. It requires you to look harder for more business—More activity every day. Staying true to a set schedule. Reading more about your craft and improving your skills. Attending more training. Attending and presenting at more meetings. Building COIs. Growing your brand. Visiting every "planet" in the Universe of Opportunities.

Making appointments for yourself to make appointments for yourself. Not giving up until you've answered three objections. Being competitive. Feeding the pipeline every single day. Learning your sales cycle. Fueling up every morning. Controlling your activity because you can't control the buyer. Asking more and better questions. Making gatekeepers allies. Building relationships with your clients, not transactions. Cold-calling in person, over the phone, via email, mail, and carrier pigeon if you have to. Not letting rejection suppress you. Asking successful sales reps lots of questions on how they do things. Not worrying about "no-shows." Outworking everyone around you. Becoming part of that 25 percent that do and leaving the 75 percent that don't! Enjoying the ride on the road less traveled by as it will have made all the difference.

In conclusion, I want to wish you the most success possible in your journey through this wonderful world of sales. Nothing, with few exceptions, is as exhilarating as that person looking across the desk from you and saying, "Yes. I would like to move forward and take advantage of what you have to offer." That's what we are striving to hear as many times as we can.

I also find it noteworthy that it feels about as good whether it was a one-location small business or a multilocation big business. Sure, the revenue and commissions were different. But just winning that "yes" feels the same to me. The hardest part of sales is getting the right person, at the right time, and under the right conditions. You need these three essentials in various parts of the process to get the appointment, to have the meeting, to get the financials or appropriate documents, to get the contracts signed, and to implement the service or use the products.

If someone could figure out how to get those three factors together whenever they wanted, that person would become extremely wealthy. The fact is, that is impossible to predict. The only solution to that is? Come on. Say it out loud with me: *activity*!

You and you alone control this. Why are my sales not as much this month as they were last month? Lack of activity. Why is our pricing not seeming competitive? Lack of activity. Why can I never beat Sheila on the sales board? Lack of activity. Why am I stressed about my goals every month? Lack of activity. Why is my manager always on me? Lack of activity.

The more activity you do, the less these things become roadblocks. John Gehegan taught me this at an early stage in my sales career: "The more prospects you have, the *less pressure* you put on yourself and them. The fewer prospects you have, the *more pressure* you put on yourself and them. He's absolutely right.

All the things we've covered in this book are built on one premise: You are willing to do the activity. Successful salespeople are the hardest working salespeople. There isn't a magic potion or a "genius salesperson gene" certain people are born with! Some of my best salespeople actually seemed kind of quiet, almost shy. They were organized, prepared, and practiced. Nothing in the real sales process comes easy; nothing. However, I am quite confident that if you stay diligent in your efforts, you will begin to reach new heights. That is my hope for you! I know you can do it! I trust a few things you've read will help you along the way. Happy selling. Increase your activity. Don't give up! Take the road less traveled.

About the Author

Chris Lovett, author of Sales People Think They Know Everything, resides in Orlando, Florida, with his wife, Stephanie, and their six children. He is a graduate of Stetson University with a BA in communications.

Chris has been a salesperson, sales manager, district manager, corporate trainer, keynote speaker and—since 1992—has trained over sixty thousand sales professionals and managers in North America. His true passion is to help others succeed and achieve greatness in their career in sales.

Lightning Source UK Ltd.
Milton Keynes UK
UKHW020851270123
416051UK00011B/147